ALSO

(Just As Well) It's Not About The Bike

ESCAPE TO CALIFORNIA

MISADVENTURES IN
AMERICA'S GOLDEN STATE

CHRIS ATKIN

Escape to California
Misadventures in America's Golden State

First edition. ISBN: 978-1-8384485-4-7

www.chrisatkinonline.com

To Wanda

CONTENTS

Climb the mountains and get their good tidings. Nature's peace will flow into you as sunshine flows into trees. The winds will blow their own freshness into you and the storms their energy, while cares will drop off like autumn leaves.

— JOHN MUIR

Big Lagoon

YREKA

EUREKA

REDDING

GRAEAGLE

MENDOCINO

Anderson Valley

Lake Tahoe

BODEGA BAY

SACRAMENTO

SONOMA

SAN FRANCISCO

Mono Lake

Yosemite

PALO ALTO

SAN JOSE

Mammoth Lakes

FRESNO

Kings Canyon

MONTEREY

Pinnacles

Death Valley

Big Sur

BAKERSFIELD

TEHACHAPI

Mojave Desert

LOS ANGELES

Channel Islands

SAN DIEGO

CALIFORNIA
UNITED STATES OF AMERICA

She pleaded our case and answered the customary questions to prove ours was not the convenience marriage it was later accused of being. When we first gave notice the year before, Sarah had panicked when asked for her job title. Fearing I wouldn't accurately recall it, she provided a simplified answer. So my subsequent 'incorrect' response about her role raised eyebrows.

This time around we were pitch perfect.

While Sarah spoke to the registrar, I remained in the waiting room, pretending not to listen. A heavily pregnant woman was seated opposite, doing likewise while her partner was cross-examined in an adjoining office. Our mutual desperation almost, but not quite, managed to overpower the inexplicable smell of cat food that clung to the peeling walls.

Giving notice should be an exciting step on the road to marriage. But weeks of despair had extinguished the romance of the occasion. Now all we wanted was a piece of paper.

Photos from our wedding day show the relief etched across our faces. We put our house up for rent and attended an emergency visa appointment at the US embassy.

One morning in early September we arrived at Heathrow Airport and walked bleary-eyed and full of disbelief through the empty terminal. As the plane took off, I had a last, lingering look back at the green fields of England before they were engulfed in cloud. I started watching *Little Women* and was soon weeping uncontrollably. Each passenger's carbon footprint must have been horrendous, but I was pleased so few people were onboard to see my tears. Sarah knows I have a propensity to cry at films, but even she was taken aback. Perhaps it was the altitude.

1

SUNRISE IN SILICON VALLEY

I awoke early with jet lag that first morning in California. Between the slats of the blinds in our hastily booked Airbnb, the sky had an unmistakable orange hue and I privately congratulated myself for having the good fortune to witness such a spectacle.

It was certainly preferable to the welcome we had received at the airport, where we were escorted by immigration officers to a separate room and ordered to remain there without explanation. By the time we were given the all-clear, I was convinced we'd be on the next plane home.

Instead, we advanced to pick up our two rucksacks, the sum total of our possessions for our life in America. They were the only items in the cavernous baggage hall, and I was relieved their sorry appearance hadn't been flagged as a security risk during our detainment.

I stayed in bed for half an hour, revelling in the possibilities that lay ahead. International borders had slammed shut, yet here we were on the other side of the Atlantic.

"Eurgh. What time is it?" Sarah asked, face down on the mattress.

"7:20."

"Good. I'm going back to sleep then."

"You're missing an amazing sunrise."

"Mmm..." Sarah mumbled, pulling the duvet over her head.

When Sarah belatedly accepted 20 minutes later that she never would get back the hours of sleep she'd lost on the flight, she too turned to see the sky. Far from having missed the display, the intensity of the orange light had only intensified. It was unlike anything we'd seen before.

The first indication something wasn't right was when our phones showed only smoke for the day's weather forecast. We didn't know such a setting even existed.

California was in the grip of its worst ever wildfire season, contending with five of the seven largest blazes in the state's history. The light show they produced continued for much of the day. Briefly a lurid yellow, the sky turned to burned apricot as we walked into town to buy some essentials.

We assumed these colours were a common side effect of the wildfires and, not wanting to reinforce British stereotypes, we resolutely avoided mentioning the unfolding drama above us. Yet it became clear the glowing sky was far from normal.

"Wow, what a time to arrive," chuckled the 7-Eleven shop assistant as he looked out of the store windows. The sky still retained a hint of orange, but the accumulating cloud and smoke had now extinguished any hope of seeing natural daylight. The few pedestrians on the street walked briskly in the eerie semi-darkness.

It's notoriously difficult to stay awake long enough to acclimatise to a new time zone, but it's even more challenging when your first full day is spent in almost perpetual dusk.

The San Francisco Bay Area has not seen another day

like it since. While the air pollution was surprisingly tolerable on the date day turned to night, the air quality deteriorated rapidly in the days that followed. Residents were forced to take refuge indoors and health authorities warned people to "stay inside, keep windows and doors closed, and keep your indoor air purified."

As new arrivals, it was a steep learning curve. We quickly familiarised ourselves with Air Quality Index numbers and sources of information as to when it might be safe to go outside again.

In all likelihood, it probably wasn't much safer for us inside. Our home was far from airtight and air purifiers were out of stock due to the sudden surge in demand.

Finding a place to live near Stanford University hadn't been easy. The institution is located in Palo Alto, the birthplace of Silicon Valley and the location of the twelfth most expensive postcode in the United States. Almost half of the 100 most expensive neighbourhoods in the country are in the San Francisco Bay Area and the rankings are topped by Atherton, a town just two miles north-west of Palo Alto. NBA star Steph Curry and former deputy British prime minister, and now president of global affairs at Facebook, Nick Clegg, are both Atherton residents.

As a Fellow at the university, Sarah would be paid for the duration of the course. Initially, we had been delighted to learn Sarah's salary would be marginally higher than the amount she earned at the time in Cambridge as a medical engineer for the National Health Service. However, when we realised the exorbitant cost of living in Palo Alto - something we don't say lightly having both lived in London for a number of years - we understood the budgetary constraints we would face.

As far back as 2016, councillors in Palo Alto considered plans to provide subsidised housing for households with a combined income of less than $250,000 per year. It goes without saying Sarah and I would be living off a fraction of this amount.

To save ourselves the hassle of finding a place when we landed, we committed to a three-month tenancy on the cheapest place we could find before we left England: a small converted shed. All ours, for the bargain price of $3,000 per month.

The shed was in the garden of the main house, where a French couple lived with their newborn baby. They couldn't believe we intended to live in such a place.

In those early weeks, one of our favourite games was finding out how we could cook without fusing the power to the shed. It was like a game of Buckaroo and we quickly discovered the importance of having a torch to hand when using the kettle.

When the air quality improved, we were able to explore Palo Alto properly. For someone who likes to think they know a bit of Spanish, it took me an embarrassingly long time to appreciate the etymology of the town's name. The 'tall stick' that inspired the moniker is a 1,083-year-old coastal redwood tree that is still alive today.

Although it is classified as a city, only 65,000 people live in Palo Alto. To its detractors, it's a soulless place set up for well-heeled tech workers to enjoy overpriced food and drink in the bars and restaurants that line University Avenue. Nonetheless, while some sneer at its lack of cool, Sarah and I never tired of admiring the enormous mansions of the super-rich. Some-times we grew nostalgic for the value for money of a Boots meal deal, but our new hometown was unlike anywhere we'd lived before and doubtless would ever live again.

One of Palo Alto's earliest success stories was Hewlett-Packard and the garage where Bill Hewlett and David

Packard founded the company in 1939 still exists. Today, Google, Facebook and Apple all have their global headquarters located nearby and their growth has contributed to making Silicon Valley one of the wealthiest places in the world. Teslas were ubiquitous and neighbourhoods reverberated with the constant low hum of electric car engines, e-bikes and scooters.

The deep pockets of many of the residents - and their desire to convey their prosperity - is encapsulated by the high number of personalised vehicle registration plates we saw. These included No WIFI, 1OLDHIP and RIP NEIL. Some even featured hearts in place of letters, which can hardly help law enforcement efforts. Still, even these vehicles were easier for authorities to track than the thousands of cars we saw on the road without registration plates on the front. The trend was noticeable across several upmarket car manufacturers, but more often than not, the vehicles in question were Teslas.

The absence of plates made the cars look like prototypes and unquestionably made them seem more stylish. But all were in breach of the law. The owners risked being pulled over by the police and issued with a $196 fine every time they used their vehicle. $196 is admittedly oddly specific, yet it's just one of many examples of how surcharges lead to driving penalties that look like they've been plucked out of the air.

If first-time visitors to Stanford University are not already slightly in awe of its illustrious reputation, it becomes increasingly difficult to remain unimpressed while travelling down Palm Drive. The kilometre-long straight road is lined with 160 palm trees and connects the campus' grand entrance to the train station and downtown Palo Alto.

Cambridge and Stanford University engender similar levels of prestige on the international stage and as an outsider who has not studied at either, but lived next door to both, it was fascinating to observe the differences between them.

Stanford cannot match the 800-year history that Cambridge boasts, but its founders, Jane and Leland Stanford, endeavoured to try. Their preference for the buildings to "be like the old adobe houses of the early Spanish days" continues to inform the university's architectural design.

Moreover, while Cambridge University's colleges are spread across the city, the majority of student life at Stanford is based on campus. When meeting up with Sarah after work, I often felt like I'd cycled straight onto the pages of the university prospectus. Undergraduates sat outside coffee shops, leisurely drinking lattes, while others played beach volleyball in bikinis. It all felt a world away from Cambridge. There at least, we didn't need to look out for kamikaze raccoons while cycling home at night.

At Stanford, Sarah was one of 10 individuals on the university's Biodesign Fellowship. Working alongside engineers, doctors and surgeons from across the world, she was tasked with identifying ways to improve the provision of healthcare and invent the necessary technology to achieve it. Which does rather make my ambitions for this book pale in comparison.

Each year, the cohort is assigned a clinical area. In 2020 it was urology and nephrology. To those of you such as myself who are blissfully ignorant of most medical terms, this meant they focused on bladders, genitals and kidneys. Due to the pandemic much of the course was remote and I picked up a lot of graphic details while Sarah was sitting across the other side of the table.

The Fellows shadowed doctors and surgeons for a period of five weeks to learn about the challenges they faced and to pinpoint areas that could be improved. During one surgery Sarah noticed a man's testicles rapidly inflate with gas.

I wasn't aware this was physically possible and would have been quick to point this out. The last thing the patient needed was to wake up to find his genitals had burst. Sarah was too embarrassed to say anything though and when the testicles reached the size of a football - a football! - the surgeon casually strolled over to them, placed them between his hands and squeezed all the air back out. Needless to say, the surgery was a success and the man never learned the source of his newfound courage.

Erectile dysfunction was swiftly identified as an issue that warranted further attention. I was incorrectly under the impression that such difficulties were solved with blue pills, but apparently they only resolve the problem for some men. One day, I returned from the shops to hear a global expert on the topic discussing his findings with Sarah's colleagues over Zoom.

"...most men regard one minute of erection as sufficient. Two minutes is considered good and five minutes is excellent."

I shot Sarah a look as I unpacked the cereal. She acknowledged it, but didn't trust herself while on video not to betray her reaction.

The 10 Fellows on the course had been broken down into two groups of five and while one of the other people on Sarah's team was a woman, she wasn't available for the debrief that immediately followed the call. As a result, it was left to Sarah to argue how long it was reasonable to expect an erection to last. This is a delicate conversation to have with your closest friends and not one you'd choose to have over Zoom with three men you barely know.

"How about we say the solution must provide an erection for 20 minutes?" she suggested.

"20 minutes? No way!" replied one of her colleagues, who, for his sake, will remain nameless. "Anything longer than 15 minutes and I need a calendar invite."

By this point, I'd finished putting the shopping away and was quietly sniggering in the kitchen. I wondered what I could say that would embarrass Sarah the most.

While Sarah was standing up for women's needs, I began looking for a secondhand car to buy. I was reluctant to buy a vehicle from a private seller online because a few years earlier I had been a victim of attempted assault while trying to purchase a bike in similar circumstances. However, our options were limited. It was too expensive to buy a car from a dealership or to rent a vehicle every time we needed one, so I agreed to meet a private owner.

The owners turned out to be a friendly Italian couple in their thirties, but I was still as jumpy as microwaved popcorn. They suggested I take the car for a test drive, which was exactly what I'd feared they would say.

Driving on the other side of the road in a car you've never been in before is always stressful, and this was amplified by the fact the car's owners were watching on intently. In the rear-view mirror, I could see their apprehension rising as I struggled to start the car. Pieces of the decaying black plastic rubbed off the steering wheel and into my sweaty hands as I tried to compose myself. Having checked the mirrors countless times, I indicated, jerked forwards and hurtled across the empty road into a cul-de-sac. Out of view, I quickly tried to test as many things as I could. Like any car though, its idiosyncrasies would only be revealed in time.

Optimistic that it might get us from A to B, I bought the car for $2,000. We were now in possession of a silver Pontiac Sunfire. If you're not sure what it looks like, that's not surprising. The manufacturer stopped making them the year it came out and the Pontiac brand ceased to exist altogether a few years after that. Its credentials to one day be regarded as a classic car are impeccable. Indeed, when we later provided details of our vehicle to a ranger in one of California's state parks, he laughed and said, "We don't get many of those around here".

In much the same way that we loved Palo Alto even though so much of it contrasted with our natural inclinations, we loved our 'new' car too. The Sunfire is a compact car that is far sportier than it is practical. It had racing stripes, race car-style seats stuck in a ludicrously reclined position, and an inexplicable sticker on the side which, at our best guess, is an unintelligible slogan in Thai. The car was 15 years old and already had 141,000 miles on the clock. It was our key to the great outdoors.

2

CALAVERAS

Sarah's colleagues arranged a weekend camping trip as an early bonding session. Our destination was Tuttletown, a three-and-a-half hour drive away to an area north-west of Yosemite National Park.

Other than overhearing them discuss sexual performance over Zoom, I had only met a couple of Sarah's colleagues before and I wasn't sure what to expect from a weekend with a bunch of overachieving strangers.

Assembling a group of high-flyers can lead to complications. The university had acknowledged as much and had appointed a psychologist to work with the teams throughout the year. They hoped that by doing so, they could preemptively address any discord that might damage the group dynamics. This hardly filled me with confidence going into the weekend.

During the Fellowship's selection process, the psychologist asked Sarah to draw a picture of her life. I'm not sure what he made of the fact I didn't feature in the image.

I needn't have worried about my fellow campers. They were reassuringly normal, even if their passion for heart stents was not. On Saturday morning I was given responsibility for planning an impromptu hike. Without phone signal or a map, this felt like a recipe for disaster, but thankfully everyone made it back alive from Calaveras Big Trees State Park.

Often overlooked in favour of Yosemite, Calaveras had the major advantage of not requiring a reservation at the time. Still, it was a 40-minute drive and I was feeling the pressure. *This walk had better be worth it.* I hadn't yet grasped the distances many Americans are willing to travel. Some would think nothing of driving that far for a coffee.

We were promised 'Big Trees' and the park features two groves of giant sequoias, the largest species of tree in the world. The cherry on the cake though was a bear sighting. I spotted it in the bushes a few metres from the path as we walked past. Plodding along on all fours, it was about the height of my thigh and, like many black bears, was brown in colour. We slowly backed off as the bear sauntered onto the narrow path, where he followed us for a while at a distance with mild curiosity.

On the drive back to our campground, we travelled through the unfortunately named town of Glory Hole. At the same time, a convoy of cars were passing through en route to a nearby rally for Donald Trump. The fervour of his followers was extraordinary. In the run-up to a general election in the UK, you don't see metre-long flags attached to people's cars in favour of a candidate. Nor do you see children running out of their houses to wave large banners promoting the virtues of an incumbent.

This behaviour hints at why the US is so politically divided. A large proportion identify as either staunchly Republican or Democrat and have been raised as such from birth. For them, candidates may come and go, but ensuring their foes from the other side of the political spectrum are prevented from entering the White House is all-important.

In the months prior to the 2020 US election, Trump's aggressive rhetoric made the US feel more divided than ever before. Politically, culturally and financially, the disparity between the country's citizens was hard to ignore. We might have been living on easy street in Palo Alto, but this didn't make it any less obvious.

California had voted in favour of the Democrats at every election since 1992 and, such was the likelihood that it would do so again, Joe Biden and Donald Trump barely made an appearance in the state while on the campaign trail. Although California has adopted much more liberal policies on issues such as the environment and abortion than have been implemented elsewhere in the country, it would be wrong to suggest these measures are universally supported by the state's citizens. After all, six million Californians voted for Trump in 2020. Whenever we drove two and a half hours east of the Pacific coast, and away from the wealth generated by Silicon Valley, we would cross the rubicon and almost immediately see placards supporting Trump. These endorsements remained long after the votes had been counted. One sticker simply read 'Trump won - we all know it'. Closer to home in leftie San Francisco, I had overheard a man say he intended to vote for Trump to try to ensure the US Supreme Court "wasn't landed with another Ruth Bader Ginsberg".

In Palo Alto nearly every house was adorned with a placard proclaiming their support for Biden. The city may be famed for its free-thinking startups, but you were just as likely to see a Trump flag there as you were a Biden banner in Glory Hole. A couple of days prior to the election I was asked to write an article describing what the atmosphere was like on the ground in Silicon Valley. The only problem was that while there were protests opposing Trump's policies elsewhere in the state, in mild, moderate Palo Alto although people were anxious, there was no sign of any unrest. Their cars and homes were too valuable for that.

I may have been unable to vote, but my personal politics were also under the microscope. Sarah's team had identified contraception as an area ripe for innovation and, given the health implications for women taking the pill, they were assessing how men could step up to the plate if they were unwilling to wear a condom. One possible answer, they decided, lay in inserting a small instrument through a man's urethra. I'm a proud feminist, but this was where I drew the line. From my reaction they quickly concluded the idea would not be commercially viable.

Men, you can thank me later.

3

HALLOWEEN

The final furlong of the US election campaign coincided, as it does every four years, with Halloween. Due to the fact we don't yet have children, and are rarely invited to Halloween fancy dress parties now we're in our thirties, in the UK we'll often just mark the event by buying a pumpkin.

We knew things would be different in the US and we weren't disappointed.

Six weeks before Halloween the supermarket aisles turned orange. In an attempt to do justice to the level of commitment made to this seasonal celebration, below is a diet you could easily 'enjoy' throughout September and October in the States.

Breakfast

Pumpkin O's - a bizarre tasting twist on Cheerios

Lunch

Pumpkin bagels - fun, but excessively sweet

Pumpkin spiced hummus and **pumpkin tortilla chips** - you'll need the former to override the unwelcome accompanying cinnamon seasoning of the latter

Pumpkin spice yoghurt - a gelatinous, flesh-coloured gloop that is best avoided

Dinner

Starter - **homemade pumpkin soup**, sprinkled with roasted **pumpkin seed**

Main - a slice of **roasted pumpkin** (difficult to fit in a toaster oven, so watch it closely to avoid burning the house down), washed down with **'Howling Gourds' pumpkin ale** (it's 7% - drink it slowly to avoid a frightening hangover)

Dessert - **pumpkin pie**, an American classic

I'm yet to convince Sarah to make Pumpkin Diet Day an annual event, but I nearly completed the menu on a couple of occasions myself. I was saved from suffering the same fate as Cinderella's carriage by an unlikely source.

As is the case in any new country, finding affordable, healthy food we could cook at home was a vital part of the acclimatisation process. The absence of a conventional oven complicated matters, but help came in the form of aubergines. These eggplants, as Americans call them, bore little similarity to aubergines in the UK. Back home, their elongated and slightly bulbous shapes mean the connotations associated with the emoji make sense. In the US, these vegetables (which are technically fruit) look nothing like the phalluses Sarah was studying. These aubergines were more like oversized bricks and a blow to the head would send you sprawling to the floor. Previously, I'd always been fairly ambivalent about the vegetable (sorry, fruit) but I quickly came to my senses when I realised that an aubergine could feed us for several days for a third of the price of a loaf of bread.

Unfortunately, due to Covid-19 trick or treating was strongly discouraged, but it seemed highly unlikely any children would have been brave enough to find the shed where we were staying in the back garden anyway. Instead, our hopes for seeing an American Halloween extravaganza lay firmly in the seasonal goodwill, wealth and materialistic one-upmanship of Palo Alto's residents. By mid-October the neighbourhood was cloaked with decorations of spider webs, ghosts and skeletons.

Illuminated witches' hats hung from the roofs of the first, second and third floor of our favourite house. Its white picket fence was adorned with plastic pumpkins and the path to the front door was lined with gourds. The centre-piece though, was the largest pumpkin we'd ever seen. If you removed the pulp, Sarah and I could both have crawled inside.

"Wow, it's amazing," said Sarah.

"It's incredible," I concurred. "All it needs is a black–"

My head turned as I heard a tinkling bell in the bushes next to us.

"Oh my God, it's actually got one too! Look, it's a black cat."

As if on cue, a cat emerged from the darkness into the orange light generated by the fairy lights wrapped around the trees in the garden. The bell on his collar continued to tinkle as he walked past the pumpkin, meowing as he approached us.

"Do you think they hire the cat each year?" Sarah asked.

"They've got it trained pretty well if they do. That's one way to beat the competition - make your Halloween decorations interactive."

The cat's desire for affection was either part of its virtuoso performance or a possible indication that it received rather less attention from its owners during the rest of the year. A worrying thought crossed my mind.

"You don't think this cat might not be black, do you?"

"What do you mean?"

"Well, maybe he's a ginger cat that gets sprayed this colour every year."

"Don't say that!"

"It's possible. The people who live here are *really* into Halloween. If they're prepared to pay for a crane to install a pumpkin that weighs around 200kg, are you sure they're beyond spraying their own cat?" I looked for a tell-tale fleck of ginger in his coat. He just stared back at me, bemused, wondering why I had stopped stroking him.

We returned a week later to see the display again. Not content with the focal point of their decorations, the owners had commissioned a sculptor to turn the pumpkin into a massive snail. But much to our disappointment, the cat wasn't anywhere to be seen. I dearly hoped he was out riding a broomstick while chasing mice, and hadn't just gone back to the rescue centre for another year.

4

SONOMA

Our first major outing in the car was to one of California's famous wine regions. We'd been warned off going to Napa due to the high prices and opted to go instead to neighbouring Sonoma, another town just over an hour's drive north of San Francisco that is renowned for its vineyards.

We enjoyed a few weekends exploring different wine regions and it never ceased to surprise us the extent to which the experiences varied. Sometimes you would have a sommelier telling you in intricate detail all the flavours we should be able to taste, while at others, staff would give you a flight of wine and allow you to blindly get on with it. Our ability to identify the flavours improved over time as we dedicated ourselves to the task. Invariably though, every red wine just tasted of plum after the equivalent of a bottle and a half of wine each. I came to terms with the fact I lacked the delicate palate (never mind the bank balance) necessary to be a connoisseur, but I endeavoured to give the impression I was a discerning drinker and I'm proud to say I now know my 'zins' from my 'cabs'.

While savouring a sample of cabernet sauvignon, we

watched in a mixture of astonishment and dismay as a middle-aged man next to us ran through a succession of wines. After tasting each, he unceremoniously poured the remaining contents of his glass into the metallic dump bucket on his table. He then beckoned the waiter over.

"I'll have a Balthazar of the 2012 Pinot Noir."

"Very well."

"Make sure the dust is kept on the bottle this time."

The waiter returned from the storeroom with a bottle that looked like it belonged on a table for giants. He gripped the neck tightly and the bottom of the bottle moved like a seismograph needle as he struggled to carry it.

The sommelier later told us the vessel contained the equivalent of 16 bottles of wine and cost $4,000. So the waiter could be forgiven for prioritising the safe arrival of the Balthazar over the loss of a little dust. Meanwhile, the man who had placed the order watched impassively as the precious cargo was placed into a box and into the boot of his blue and neon orange Tesla.

It was fun imagining what it would be like to turn up at a house party with such an oversized bottle. Yet witnessing the lack of fanfare that accompanied this extravagant purchase demonstrated that, try as I might, I'd never fit in with some of the wine country's clientele.

Neither Sarah nor I ever volunteered to stay sober when visiting vineyards. Watching the other eulogise about the merits of each wine would be too painful. Taxis either didn't exist or were prohibitively expensive, so it was necessary to walk from one vineyard to the next. This sounds idyllic, but the reality was rather different. With a few notable exceptions, the wineries in most towns were usually found along the main road. In the absence of pavements, we were forced to share the asphalt with the cars as they sped perilously close to us at more than 60mph. This was never pleasant, but we spotted things we wouldn't otherwise have noticed. For example, we once saw eight vultures standing on separate posts next to us at one end of a vineyard, all appearing to wait in line for their turn to pick at the carrion of a deer hit by a car.

We hoped there would at least be safety in numbers when walking along the road. Yet we never saw anyone else undertaking a similar vineyard crawl to us. Some groups had bullied or bribed an individual to be the designated driver, but judging by those around us, many customers were drink-driving. The police are apparently aware of the problem, but we never saw any authorities doing anything about it.

Sometimes the vineyards were a couple of miles apart and, having dodged the drink-drivers, we often arrived feeling like we'd earned our pit stop.

At a large wooden barn we were greeted by a sommelier ready to practise her well-rehearsed description of the tasting menu. But before she could begin, Sarah pointed at a strange-looking contraption on one of the bottles on the bar.

"Is that a Coravin?"

"Yes, it is," said the surprised sommelier.

"Oh wow! The director on my course co-invented that."

"They're great. We would be lost without them. They save us from having to waste so much wine."

"Hang on, what is it?" I interjected.

"It allows us to keep open bottles of wine for a number of years without worrying about the risk of oxidisation," the woman explained.

Sarah and the woman proceeded to discuss the device in great detail. First it inserts a needle into the cork to allow the wine to be poured. Then it replaces the extracted wine with Argon gas to keep the remaining wine fresh. I should have guessed an engineer and a sommelier would have a shared interest in such an object.

When visiting Sonoma, we spent Sundays exploring the local countryside. During our first trip we visited a state park established on land once owned by Jack London, author of *The Call of the Wild*. London was a maverick adventurer and one of the most romantic figures of the early 20th century. A restless soul who had been lucky to survive his mother's failed suicide attempt when he was in utero, London belatedly found an element of peace and stability in rural Sonoma. His dream house burned down just prior to its completion and was never rebuilt as London died three years later at the age of 40. The remnants of the house remain, but it is the views over the rolling hills of perfectly symmetrical rows of vines that capture the imagination.

On another Sunday, we travelled nine miles north of London's former home to Sugarloaf Ridge. Wildfires in 2017 and 2020 destroyed thousands of acres of land in the region, leaving only 1% of the state park unscathed. The hillside was full of scorched trees and their fractured branches lay scattered across the ground. Considering much of this damage occurred barely six months before we visited the park, it was remarkable how green - albeit at low level - the scenery was and how quickly nature was bouncing back.

The difference in the appearance of the vineyards throughout the year was noticeable too. When we first visited in autumn, the leaves were still green and the vines heavy with plump grapes. In early spring their growth had been cut back. Stripped of their fecund creepers, the plants looked barren and naked. The visual impact of this was soft-ened in some vineyards by the sowing of bright yellow mustard plants. Mustard is an ideal cover crop for winemakers. Its deep roots prevent soil erosion and, because the plant produces high levels of biofumigants, it suppresses the population of microscopic worms known as nematodes that damage the vines. Its yellow flowers also attract beneficial insects, and more conspicuously, large numbers of Instagrammers who flock to lie among the flowers.

5

A BIRTHDAY SURPRISE

Weeks rushed past in a blur as we settled into our new lives. I even began to accept hearing people call autumn 'Fall', though I couldn't bring myself to do so. 'Cab' and 'zin' might be amusingly pretentious, but Fall was just too literal. And if you're thinking it's now November, it's winter anyway, it certainly didn't feel like it. The sunshine the Bay Area receives has the effect of an accordion on the seasons, extending late spring, summer and early autumn into one glorious period almost devoid of rain, and truncating late autumn, winter and early spring into a few condensed weeks.

On one mid-November weekend we celebrated the birthday of one of Sarah's colleagues by going for a group walk. We started near Mori Point, a 20-minute drive south of San Francisco and the location of a notorious speakeasy during Prohibition. Heading inland from the coast, we walked up to Sweeney Ridge. The hilltop has historical significance as the place from which Gaspar de Portolá became the first European to see San Francisco Bay in 1769. On the day of our hike though, it was simply a good place to eat cake.

Continuing beyond the three miles we'd walked to reach the summit would lead us back to the car park, but most of the group favoured taking the more direct route down the hill we'd just climbed.

Sarah and I always preferred to do loop walks when possible, rather than simply hiking out and back. We assumed everyone felt the same. But nearly every American we spoke to was at best ambivalent about which was better. Maybe our preference marked us out as British, or perhaps it's one of those quirks every couple has where something that seems obvious to them, marks them out as odd to everyone else.

At the risk of appearing anti-social, the pair of us opted to keep going. We soon heard loud, continuous shouting up ahead, and as we reached the crest of a large dip in the hillside we saw for the first time where it was coming from. On the opposite crest, about 50 metres away, a young family appeared on bicycles yelling incomprehensibly. We guessed this was part of a harmless, if slightly obnoxious, game to keep the young boy and girl on the bikes entertained. Except no one looked like they were having fun. The mother rode straight past us at high speed, closely followed by her two screaming children.

The father paused only briefly when he reached us.

"We've just seen a mountain lion on the hillside. The noise seemed to scare him away, but we lost sight of him. I'd turn back if I was you."

I bit my lip as I considered our options. Sarah's colleagues would be too nice to say anything, but going back to the group with our tail between our legs would be embarrassing. Worse still would be if they came to the conclusion that we had lied about intending to go another way so that Sarah and I could walk behind them alone.

"How dangerous is it?" I asked.

"You'll be safe when you get near the town, but if you keep going, stay close to each other and make a lot of noise. Good luck." He headed off to catch up with his children, leaving us in a cloud of dust and uncertainty. Loitering where we were while we deliberated what to do clearly wasn't sensible, so Sarah and I made loud noises as we continued down the hill.

After bellowing for more than a minute, I realised that a constant, drawn-out shout was really just providing an annoying background noise and wasn't likely to deter a mountain lion. Genuinely terrified of being attacked from behind and clawed to pieces, I wracked my brain for more varied sounds. I sounded like R2D2 at his most animated, so I turned to singing. In my panic to avoid silence, the only song I could remember the words to was *Happy Birthday*. I'm certain my cover version, a sort of angry staccato, was a new take on the classic.

We walked as briskly downhill as we could manage across the rocky terrain, recalling the lyrics to as many songs as we could remember. Having gone through everything from Abba to The Zutons, I finally thought of a noise certain to frighten any animal. I started yodelling.

It's telling that Sarah didn't laugh at any of these antics. She'd busied herself by hitting two large sticks together, replicating a technique she recalled seeing on *The Parent Trap*.

When we were a mile down the trail we relaxed a little, confident that my yodelling had seen off the mountain lion. The sun was setting over the white buildings on the peninsula and the idyllic view out to sea looked like it had been lifted from a Greek travel brochure.

Since passing the cyclists we hadn't seen anyone else, which suggested either the mountain lion had got to them first, or that they'd heard my yodelling and turned back home. The mountain lion also remained thankfully elusive. This begs the question whether the family had been playing a game all along.

All I know for sure is that I woke up the next morning with a sore throat.

6

THANKSGIVING

The following weekend was Thanksgiving. Eager to make the most of the holiday, we set off to the Sierra Nevada with two of Sarah's colleagues, Victoria and Susanna.

Our first stop was Mono Lake, one of the oldest lakes in North America and certainly one of the most unique. In the 1930s the hot springs on the islands led the destination to be billed the 'Tahiti of the Sierras'. This is at odds with Mark Twain's experience 70 years earlier. He described the area as a "lifeless, treeless, hideous desert" and the "loneliest place on Earth". Unsurprisingly, his description isn't referenced by the region's tourism board.

Standing almost completely alone in the desolate terrain, the sense of isolation felt as uncomfortable as it was inescapable. I've never been to Tahiti, but I'd bet Lake Mono is closer to Twain's description than any part of French Polynesia.

Mono Lake covers an area of 70 square miles and lies in a vast, flat expanse encircled by mountains and ancient volcanoes. The rain shadow behind these peaks has made the basin an arid, featureless landscape. As a result, distances were difficult to estimate. After a longer than anticipated walk in the cold, crisp air, we arrived at a collection of 30ft high white stone towers at the water's edge.

These *tufa* are caused by the lake's salinity, which is nearly three times higher than that of seawater. Trapped by the area's topography, the water in Mono Lake has no route to the sea. Dissolved salts and calcium accumulate rapidly and when freshwater springs meet the lake's alkaline waters, a chemical reaction occurs, creating spires of calcium carbonate. While tufa are a natural phenomena, their exposure above the lake's surface is not. Rather, it's a consequence of drought and eight decades spent diverting water 300 miles south to service Los Angeles' citizens.

In spite of its inhospitable appearance, the lake retains huge ecological importance. Two million annual migratory birds feed on the endemic shrimp in the lake and an astonishing 85% of California's seagulls are believed to have hatched here.

Returning to the car, we drove 20 minutes south towards June Lake Loop. It was our first experience of a particular type of stereotypically American tourist attraction. Running adjacent to the main road, the 16-mile route primarily exists to enable drivers and passengers to see the magnificent scenery without the inconvenience of getting out of the car. We'd anticipated the road would be closed this late in the season, but conveniently for us the year's first heavy snowfall had yet to arrive. We hadn't earned the views, but skirting the turquoise alpine lakes as the sun slipped behind the snow-dusted peaks in the late afternoon was undeniably magical.

The paucity of snow on the ground, combined with the irresistible beauty of the landscape we had driven through, prompted me to convince the others to commit to an 18-mile hike into the mountains the next day. Given we had fewer than 10 hours of daylight to complete the 4,000ft climb this was an ambitious undertaking, but I assured them they wouldn't regret it.

I didn't wish to show it, for fear they would suggest an alternative, more moderate route, but I did harbour some reservations myself. I knew Sarah would be able to match me step for step, and Victoria and Susanna had gone hiking before, but we weren't sure what the conditions would be like in the mountains. We didn't have any poles, crampons or ice picks. We didn't even have hiking trousers. I'd be wearing the one pair of trousers I had brought with me to the States: a pair of jeans.

After scraping the ice off the windscreen in the dark at 6.30am, we drove 20 minutes to the trailhead and began our ascent into the Ansel Adams Wilderness. Sunlight crept gradually down the face of the mountains and the untouched, crystallised snow began to sparkle around us. The area was renamed in memory of the acclaimed American photographer shortly after his death in 1984. Adams spent much of his life documenting the Sierra Nevada and it's easy to see why the region had such a profound effect on him. It was nearly impossible to take a bad photograph.

As we marvelled at the views, we came across a rail track running up the mountain that was almost completely submerged by snow. Built more than a century ago, it was a staggering feat of engineering, designed to move equipment to the hydroelectric plants at two of the lakes above us. The track took a direct route to the top, but following it would have led to an even faster descent to the valley floor.

We stuck to the switchbacks and stopped at Lake Agnew for a breakfast of pre-prepared porridge, feeling smug for seizing the day and congratulating ourselves for the progress we had already made. However, the depth of the snow increased as we climbed above the lake and questions began to be asked, only half in jest, about how sensible it was to keep going. The map indicated that the route zigzagged up the steep hillside, but without crampons, our boots simply slid off the ice sheets that covered the snow, causing us to skid down the mountain. To avoid this, I stamped into the snow, creating deep footprints like inverted islands for the others to use behind me. I just had to remember to shorten my stride so they didn't become stranded.

Occasionally, I'd stick my foot through a snow bank and find myself stuck, knee-deep in snow. It was at these moments I felt particularly vulnerable. For although the bears were hibernating, the mountain lions and wolves were not.

The route disappeared entirely as we ascended to 10,000ft. No one had walked here for weeks and we were beginning to realise why. Even the views of the pine-covered mountains against the bright blue sky couldn't disguise the fact morale was dropping. While I was starting to feel the effects of acting as a human snow plough, Victoria was regretting wearing ankle socks. Shocked by the unrelenting cryogenic therapy, her ankles had turned a disturbing shade of luminescent orange.

We reached a meadow buried under a thick blanket of pristine snow. Somewhere deep beneath our feet, the trail traversed the grassland, but finding it would be guesswork. We collapsed into the snow as Sarah pulled out some home-made chocolate cookies for what she subsequently described as the "most important cookie stop ever". In America we regularly bit off more than we could chew, so that's quite a statement. Perhaps I didn't realise quite how close the group had come to mutiny.

Susanna and Victoria were too nice to say it, but I knew from Sarah's eyes that if I was to stave off a vote of no confidence, concessions needed to be made. Everyone's toes were swimming in icy water and our fingers had long since turned numb in our gloves. We hastily amended the route to make it five miles shorter.

After crossing the meadow, we passed a succession of small frozen lakes emitting unnerving, sonorous groans as the ice thawed and cracked in the sunshine. The descent began through a glade of trees scarred with notches to show us the way. Having not come across this navigation tool before, we initially assumed these were wildlife markings and it was some time before we came to the happy realisation of the abrasions' true purpose.

This side of the mountain received more sun exposure, but this was a double-edged sword. In some places pools of snowmelt had repeatedly frozen overnight, creating sections of black ice over the shoulder-width stone path. I teased Sarah at first for crossing these parts like a crab, but I soon appreciated that it was better than falling 300ft down the scree into Lake Agnew.

Darkness was starting to fall when we returned to the car. The bottom of my jeans had frozen in the snow and when we returned to our chalet I discovered they had acted like sandpaper over the course of the day, rubbing off the hair on my calves. I looked like a professional cyclist who had chickened out of waxing his legs halfway through. Nothing could be done for my svelte calves now, but we promised to lend Victoria some full-length socks the following day.

~

Climbing to the top of Reversed Peak required scrambling over rocks, but it was much easier than the day before. We passed only patches of snow, making it easy to follow the gravel paths through the low-lying chaparral. Looking south and west from the summit, we admired the serrated edges of the Sierra Nevada and compared the sizes of the four bodies of water encompassed by June Lake Loop. Mono Lake was visible to the north, its scale finally perceptible as we stood 3,000ft above it.

Just inside the state border to the east stood the White Mountains. Separating us from these mountains was a wide valley, through which Highway 395 ran like a thread. Underneath this plateau is the Long Valley Caldera, which was identified in 2018 as one of the world's largest supervolcanoes.

To begin with we were alone at the peak, but it soon became clear this local vantage point was a magnet for unorthodox individuals. First, two women in their late twenties appeared, looking like they'd lost something.

"Have you seen a tin can?"

"Yes I have," I replied, as surprised that I was able to help, as I was confused by the question.

One of the women bent down to where I had pointed and fetched the rusty can. It reminded me of the old baked bean tin my dad keeps at the end of the garden, which he uses for toilet breaks to enrich the compost.

The pencil and paper that fell out of the can suggested this one served a different purpose. The woman neatly wrote down her and her companion's names, put the pencil and paper back in the can and returned it to where she found it. The two of them looked at the scenery for less than a minute, shrugged, and slowly set off again.

Shortly afterwards, we were joined by a different type of peak-bagger. A wiry man in his fifties arrived at the summit with a pole sticking out the top of his bag. His companion, a younger, much stockier man, arrived a few minutes later, breathing heavily and carrying a big rucksack. I was chat-

7

SAN FRANCISCO

We made our second visit to San Francisco on the first weekend of December. Eager to familiarise ourselves with the city to the extent we felt comfortable calling it SF, our initial trip had taken place within the first few weeks of our arrival. I had visited once before, almost a decade earlier, so I'd led Sarah on a whistle-stop tour.

In 2021 *Time Out* named San Francisco the best city in the world. I was bowled over by it back in 2012, but was shocked, as many tourists are, by the scale of the city's homeless population. Authorities have attempted to tackle the problem for decades, but walking through the city it was clear the issue remains. One former resident who now lives in the suburbs told us they moved to avoid the discomfort of having to explain to their children why people were sleeping on cardboard boxes in the street.

As we walked hand in hand towards Chinatown from the train station, a large black woman with cropped hair approached us with animated eyes.

"Are you two a couple?"

"Yes."

"You both have perfect body shapes. You must have amazing sex."

Growing up in Britain doesn't prepare you for conversations like this. Particularly when the bit about us having perfect bodies wasn't true - neither of us had seen the inside of a gym for at least six years. As for the amazing sex...Sarah laughed. The moment passed as I searched for a suitable response. Which was probably for the best.

I don't wish to diminish the compliment, but as we walked through the city, we saw many people with mental health issues, who were cursing, screaming and shouting to themselves. I hoped these individuals were receiving the support they needed, but I didn't hold out much hope in a country where comprehensive healthcare comes at a price.

San Francisco's Chinatown is the oldest in North America and the largest Chinese enclave outside of Asia. Today, the neighbourhood attracts more visitors than the Golden Gate Bridge, but it has overcome numerous setbacks to get to this point. At the turn of the 20th century officials repeatedly sought to relocate the district to the outskirts of the city. Residents rallied against these attempts, but were powerless to stop its destruction in 1906.

On the morning of 18 April, witnesses described seeing San Francisco's streets rising and falling like a ribbon in the wind. The earthquake ignited uncontrollable fires which burned for four days, after which more than 3,000 people had died and half of the city's population was homeless.

The fire department's efforts to tame the flames were impeded by their use of dynamite to demolish buildings. They hoped the practice would create firebreaks, but often it merely sparked additional fires. The problem was exacerbated further by residents deliberately setting their houses on fire. Insurers only provided protection against fire damage, so individuals living in properties that had been rendered structurally unsound by the earthquake took matters into their own hands to qualify for compensation.

Chinatown's residents feared their homes would be relocated while they lay in ashes and their determination to avoid this fate ensured the area was one of the first to be rebuilt. As we walked through the neighbourhood, past small restaurants and shops selling fragrant herbs and spices, my eyes were drawn to the Transamerica Pyramid in the financial district. I recognised the building from one of my school textbooks, where it was used to show how engineers attempt to design skyscrapers capable of withstanding earthquakes. Charles Richter, the man who invented the scale used to measure the Earth's tremors, believed these efforts were futile in places of high tectonic activity and opposed the construction of skyscrapers anywhere in California.

For several decades San Francisco council limited the number and scale of the city's high-rise structures. This was due to aesthetic concerns as much as safety. However, the growth of Silicon Valley and the need to address the city's soaring rent prices, has led to a change of policy in recent years. When it was built in 1972, the Transamerica Pyramid was the eighth tallest skyscraper in the world. Its four-sided concrete and glass design remains iconic, but it's no longer the tallest building in the city.

On the waterfront, the arcades and souvenir shops at Fisherman's Wharf held little appeal, and in the midst of the pandemic, the tourist attraction felt like an unloved relic. There are few bleaker sights than an empty tourist pier and the contrast to my visit nine years earlier, when crowds of happy families were gathered here, was stark. The sea lions at Pier 39 did their best to entertain, but few visitors stayed for long. We ate lunch in nearby Aquatic Park, watching the open water swimmers brave the wind and cold water as they waded into the Pacific without wetsuits.

Further west is the Palace of Fine Arts. The building, modelled on Roman and Ancient Greek ruins, is the only surviving structure from the world fair held in San Francisco in 1915. Officially, the exposition was in celebration of the completed Panama Canal, but the event became a showcase for the city's post-earthquake recovery. The structures built for the world fair were intended to be demolished after the event, but public sentiment demanded that the palace, with its grand rotunda and lagoon, remained. By the 1950s the simulated ruin was itself falling apart and over a period of 10 years it was rebuilt from scratch.

We headed back to the water to gain a better view of the Golden Gate Bridge's red towers peeking through the clouds. The shoreline at Crissy Fields is a former military airfield, which, prior to the bridge's construction in the 1930s, was involved in several pioneering aviation attempts, such as the first successful dawn-to-dusk transcontinental flight across the US. In 1925 it was also the take-off site for the first attempt to fly from the continental United States to Hawaii. John Rodgers predicted his flying boat would complete the journey in 26 hours. It ended up taking nine days. When the plane ran out of fuel and landed in the sea, the crew erected fabric from the wing to use as a sail. They sailed 450 miles to Hawaii, surviving a week without food, until they were rescued 15 miles from land.

Our walk back to the train station was only five miles, but the city's unforgiving hills made it feel longer. Riding a bike here would be hard work, yet bicycles once dominated the city's roads and the mass market manufacturing of bikes in the 1890s is considered a key milestone in the campaign for women's rights. This is because bicycles gave many women the ability to navigate independently for the first time. In 1896 activist Susan B. Anthony went as far as to say that cycling "has done more to emancipate women than anything else in the world".

In order to prevent their long dresses becoming entangled in the chain or the spokes, some women took to wearing 'bloomers'. These puffy, ankle-length trousers were far more practical, but were soon subject to criticism. Detractors claimed "immorality is alarmingly on the increase among American women, and all because of the horrid bicycle".

Sadly, the popularity of the bicycle in San Francisco peaked in 1896, when an estimated 5,000 cyclists rode in front of a cheering crowd of 100,000 people to demand road improvements. The road was repaired as a result, but it was the car rather than the bike that principally benefitted.

Our second visit to San Francisco began in Golden Gate Park. At one end is the botanical gardens and at the other, three miles west, is the ocean. We were sitting under a pergola in the former when a coyote ambled across the lawn. Parents pulled their children a little closer, but most people were unperturbed. I was impressed. If a similar incident was to occur in Kew Gardens in London, people would be jumping into the Thames.

When the park was created, it was a point of pride that it was larger than New York's Central Park. Yet the idea that citizens might wish to walk from one end to another appears to have been an afterthought for the park's landscapers. We quickly became lost and repeatedly found ourselves spewed out of the tree line onto major roads such as the six-lane highway of Crossover Drive. So we were relieved when we arrived at the picturesque Dutch Windmill located by the beach.

The windmill and the neighbouring tulip garden was a gift to the city from Queen Wilhelmina of the Netherlands. Built to irrigate the park and convert the windswept sand dunes into fertile soil capable of supporting more than two million trees from around the world, it proved so successful that a second, larger windmill was constructed. Combined, the park's windmills pumped 1.5 million gallons of water per day. The development of electric pumps now fulfil this task, but the windmills and tulip garden remain as popular as ever. Not least with wedding photographers.

At the beach, we turned north to reach Lands End Trail. Not far from the start, we could see the concrete remains of Sutro Baths. Today they resemble the type of neglected open-air seawater swimming pools seen the world over, but in their heyday in the late 19th century these baths were reminiscent of a royal palace and housed the globe's largest collection of indoor swimming pools.

Further around the coast we spotted several seals near the shore. The Marin Headlands lie directly across the strait and, to the east, stands the Golden Gate Bridge. After debating the relative merits of each of the mansions in the fabulously wealthy Sea Cliff district, Sarah and I walked past the deteriorating remnants of the Presidio artillery batteries and arrived at the bridge.

At the time of its construction, many experts argued the project would never succeed, but it was finished ahead of schedule and delivered under budget. The suspension bridge's famous red colour is not, it transpires, red after all, but 'international orange'. It's difficult to imagine now, but the US Navy opposed this colour choice, preferring black and yellow to ensure the bridge could be seen by passing ships. Fortunately they were overruled, and the bridge avoided looking like it belonged in a crime scene.

The landmark fully deserves its place as one of the Seven Wonders of the Modern World. The bridge's chief engineer, Joseph Strauss, has a mixed legacy though. While he cruelly downplayed the pivotal role played by his colleagues in designing the bridge, his innovative deployment of safety nets during the construction phase saved the lives of 19 men who fell from the bridge. Together they formed the Half Way to Hell Club.

We walked across the bridge just in time to watch sunset from the Marin Headlands. Then we set off on the long walk back towards the city, watching as lights switched on and twinkled in the twilight.

Sarah had made plans for us to meet up with her university friend, Steve, and his wife that evening. As we made our way to the restaurant, I asked Sarah for some context. I've a tendency to put my foot in it, and was eager to avoid committing any faux pas when meeting these prospective new friends for the first time.

"So when was the last time you saw Steve?"

Sarah paused to consider this. "I don't know. He moved out here about two years ago and I hadn't seen him much before that."

"Is his wife British?"

"Yes, she is. She's called Lucy, I think. They moved to California together. I've never met her, but apparently she's nice."

"Is that according to Steve?"

"No," Sarah replied, elbowing me. "That's according to my friends."

"Ok. Do we know how Steve met his wife?"

"I've no idea, actually. You can ask them."

"I will. Is there anything I should know not to ask them?"

"Like what?"

"I don't know, are either of them missing an arm?"

Sarah rolled her eyes. "Steve had two arms last time I saw him. And if he doesn't any more, I reckon you'll work it out."

"Fair enough. Is there anything else I should know? Did you and Steve ever have an illicit romance?"

"No," Sarah said too quickly. "Even if we had, why would it have been illicit?"

"Is there something you want to tell me? Are you going to insist our first child is called Steve?"

"No! That would make things difficult if she was a girl. Look, Steve and I kissed. Once. Nothing else happened."

"Sarah and Steve sitting in a tree, K-I-S–"

"Oh, stop it!" Sarah interjected. "It was more than 10 years ago!"

"So you don't want me to bring it up tonight?"

"No!"

"How about I gently allude to it?

"I've never heard you gently allude to anything."

"Fine," I said, pretending to sulk. "Maybe I'll just flirt outrageously with Steve's wife. What's her name again?"

"Lucy. Right, we're here. Just try to be normal, please."

At the restaurant, only outdoor dining was permitted due to the pandemic. Steve and Lucy were running a little late and, as we sat waiting in the cold, I had to admit I was ready not to like them. My hands were so numb I was worried I wouldn't be able to hold a knife and fork.

"Hi, how are you guys? Sorry we're late," said a tall, bearded man with two arms. I presumed this to be Steve.

It was his wife that caught my attention. She was small and pretty, with brown straight hair cut into a fringe. She looked confusingly like the older sister of a girl I used to know.

I've learned it's usually best if I hold myself back from expressing the inner workings of my mind to strangers and I didn't want to scare Lucy with questions about whether she was related to someone she'd almost certainly never heard of. The uncanny resemblance puzzled me, but I began to notice she was looking strangely at me too.

"Hi, I'm Lucy." She paused. "Do I recognise you?"

"Yeah...I think you might." I realised this made it sound like I thought I was a celebrity, so I swiftly added, "I think I recognise you."

"Chris Atkin, right?"

"Yes. And you're Lucy Gold?"

"Yes! Well, I was."

"Ah thank goodness. I thought I was going mad."

Sarah and Steve were both watching us, bemused.

"Chris and I were at the same college at university together," Lucy said by way of explanation.

After an enjoyable dinner discussing the differences between the UK and the US, we returned to the car and drove home.

"So...did you have a nice evening?" Sarah asked.

"Yeah, it was fun. They're both really nice. We should definitely hang out again."

"Oh, phew. I was worried you were going to say you hated her at university."

"No, why would I say that? I didn't know Lucy well - certainly not as well as you knew Steve - but she always seemed friendly."

"I thought you might just have been keeping up appearances."

"No," I laughed. "I'm not that good an actor."

There aren't many perks to having an author for a husband. For a start, unless you have a breakout hit, the money's terrible. Moreover, my writing increasingly encroaches on Sarah's life. In my debut book, *(Just As Well) It's Not About The Bike*, Sarah is mentioned only in reference to her absence. When sharing a shed though, there is nowhere to hide.

While Sarah gives me carte blanche to write about our misadventures, it would be dangerous to assume everyone felt the same. For this reason, it was important I asked Steve and Lucy for permission to include the preceding passage. This was potentially a delicate matter for a number of reasons. Sarah had begun to doubt whether the alcohol-infused late-night kiss with Steve had actually occurred. Steve is a good-looking guy and if he didn't recall the kiss, Sarah worried it would make her look like a fantasist trying to stir up trouble. Even if Steve did confirm the event happened, we didn't know if Lucy knew.

Sarah and I were both confident Steve wouldn't suddenly use my mention of the alleged incident to confess his undying love for Sarah. Nevertheless, we were aware that dropping the topic into conversation would, for many people, be an unwelcome way to find out about your husband's past - however small a footnote it represented. So when Sarah and Lucy were briefly walking ahead of Steve and I a few months later, I saw my opportunity.

"I don't want Lucy to hear this, just in case, and if the answer is yes, of course it's absolutely fine, but I need to ask you a question."

"Sure," Steve said, intrigued by my array of caveats and sudden conspiratorial tone.

In hindsight, I should have prefaced the question with

the wider context that I was writing a book, but knowing that Lucy would soon be within earshot again, time was of the essence.

So like a man spoiling for a fight outside a pub, I asked Steve outright if he'd got with my wife.

I did try not to do it quite like that. I wanted to reassure him that in no way would I feel bitter or twisted if he had. Equally, I didn't want there to be any misunderstanding in regard to the definition of 'getting with' someone, so like a love-lorn 14-year-old, I asked "Did you kiss Sarah?".

To his credit, Steve didn't burst into laughter. Recognising the kiss for the inconsequential act it was, he replied, "Yes," openly and immediately.

"Ah, that's great," I said, relieved. "Thanks so much." I sounded like a cuckold.

8

SCHOOL'S OUT

Winter had finally arrived. In the absence of central heating, the temperature in the shed fell precipitously each night and we raced to turn the tiny electrical heater on each morning. Christmas decorations were also beginning to appear, heightening our anticipation of the festive season.

One neighbourhood had installed a 30ft high pile of giant baubles, each one nearly the size of our accommodation. Nearby, inflatable sleighs adorned roofs next to illuminated helicopters piloted by Santa and emblazoned with the words 'Operation Present Drop' on the side. Of course, we made a special visit to the house which had carved a giant pumpkin into the shape of a snail at Halloween. Our walk to the decadently decorated six-bed mansion felt like a pilgrimage to the shrine of materialism, and although we saw no sign of the cat - black or otherwise - we weren't disappointed. A 9ft tall Nutcracker statue and a giant Olaf the snowman inflatable stood alongside several Christmas trees dressed in tinsel.

Full of Christmas spirit, in the middle of December Sarah and I left Palo Alto for a few weeks. Sarah was able to work remotely during the last week of term and we both fancied living somewhere other than a shed. After three months, we would not be returning to the place we had come to call home.

Primarily, this was because we couldn't afford the rent. But tensions with the family living in the main house had arisen over recent weeks. When they signed the lease, the landlord had failed to mention that we'd shortly be moving into the garden. Understandably, they felt a little aggrieved. They remained civil, but became increasingly obstructive to ensure we weren't tempted to stay put.

We headed to Tehachapi, a small town in southern California that is home to fewer than 15,000 people. I found out too late the area is pronounced Te-Hatch-Api not Teha-Chapi and, as with the pronunciation of Hermione in *Harry Potter*, I suspect I'll never fully mentally adjust. We had chosen Tehachapi, not for any particular attraction, but because it was conveniently located to break up the journey towards our Christmas holiday destination. This seemed sensible, particularly when the sat nav told us to "continue along I-5 S for 150 miles". You don't get that kind of instruction in the UK.

As we travelled down California's Central Valley we drove past almond trees either side of the road. The surrounding plantations represent less than 1% of America's farmland, yet produce a quarter of the nation's fruit and nuts.

Periodically, tumbleweed rolled across the wide, dusty roads. I'd previously considered these dry balls of vegetation to be vaguely comical, worthy of their depiction in cartoons or their metaphorical appearance after a misjudged joke at a dinner party. But, as with many things in life, they are decidedly less amusing when driving towards them at 65mph. Suddenly, these spheres of withered plant matter didn't seem so innocuous. Some of the tumbleweed was big enough to scratch car windows, and the bent branches on even the smaller ones would have wreaked havoc to the underside of the car.

Perhaps we'd grown soft in cosseted Palo Alto, but having dodged the surprisingly fast-moving tumbleweed, when we reached Tehachapi, it felt like we'd stepped into a noir thriller. We turned off the highway in driving rain - something we hadn't seen since our arrival in the States - and negotiated our way through a series of confusing cul-de-sacs.

Our accommodation was on the outskirts of town, in a neighbourhood where every property had large propane gas canisters in the garden, pick-up trucks in the drive and was furnished with at least one ornamental owl. Very few of the houses had Christmas decorations, but we could tell people were home from the smoke emanating from the chimneys. In spite of this, during the duration of our week-long stay, we barely saw so much as a curtain twitch.

Tehatchapi's name is believed to derive from 'tihachipia', the word for 'hard climb' in the ancient Kawaiisu Native American language. Like moths to a flame, one afternoon we set off to conquer the hardest climb around, Mount Tehachapi.

As we ascended, the branches of the surrounding pine trees became increasingly weighed down by the thick icicles attached to each needle. Several icicles dropped around us in the sunshine, shattering upon impact and adding to the millions of ice shards already scattered across the frozen ground. The reflection of the sunlight in all directions was mesmerising. But it also felt like we were walking up a hill covered in marbles while under aerial attack. If one of the icicles landed on our heads, we'd have more than a trickle of frozen water running down our backs to worry about.

Through the trees, we could see patches of mist

hovering around the forested mountain peaks. It felt like we had discovered our own piece of Narnia. The illusion disappeared when we came across private property signs near the summit. This was not the first time we had followed a route on a map, only to be confronted by 'Keep Out' signs. Often, we were left with no alternative but to return the way we'd come. On one particularly memorable occasion, we were met by a sign that read:

If you're seen in here today, your body will be found
here tomorrow

Clearly, these landowners weren't messing around.

That it had been considered acceptable to sell off land at the top of a mountain almost 8,000ft high and allow a 600ft perimeter fence to be erected around it was deplorable.

Quite sure we were alone, Sarah and I stepped over the low-lying barbed wire fence. We braced ourselves for the firing of a warning shot - assuming there would at least be one - and made our way to the peak. No one else was there, but we chose not to stay for long and decided it was best to quit while we were ahead. A trip to the local German bakery beckoned and we skated our way down the icy slope for a well-deserved pastry.

On the drive back, we noticed a house with red fairy lights across its roof. As I drove closer, I could see they spelled 'TRUMP' in large letters. We doubted the home-owners would appreciate our interest, but I couldn't resist asking Sarah to take a photo. Against her better judgement, she did so. We then headed off at speed before we could become acquainted with the owner's shotgun.

9

THE MOJAVE DESERT

At the end of our week in Tehachapi, our Christmas road trip began in earnest. The first stop was the Mojave Desert, or more specifically the Mojave National Preserve, as the desert comprises areas as far afield as Joshua Tree National Park and Death Valley.

The only crowd we'd seen in Tehachapi was the queue for the bakery, yet we were still taken aback by the vast emptiness of the desert. Electrical pylons running parallel to the long, straight roads were the only sign of human presence. Rocky hills loomed in the distance, but surrounded by the sparsely vegetated plateau, their scale was incalculable.

After driving east for three hours, we pulled over at Kelso Dunes. The dunes are among the largest in the country, but after our training over Thanksgiving, I expected our walk to the summit to be little more than a chance to stretch our legs.

I'd forgotten how difficult it is to walk in deep sand.

The dunes seemed perpetually stuck on the horizon, and even when we reached them, we needed to pause regularly on their slopes to catch our breath.

Upon reaching the top of the 200m dune, we took off

our boots and socks and enjoyed sinking our feet into the hot sand. Having secured the boots to the rucksack, we threw ourselves back downhill. On the steep incline we quickly gathered momentum and it was hard to stay upright.

Amid the jubilation, I could feel strange vibrations against my heel and, over the sound of the boots knocking into each other at my back, I could hear a sound similar to that of a low-flying plane. The exact cause of this phenomenon, known as 'singing sand' or 'booming dunes', is still disputed, but Kelso Dunes is one of the few places in the world where it occurs.

Refusing to accept the limitations of the winter solstice, I tried to squeeze one more walk into the day. We'd reached the middle of Mojave National Preserve along a rapidly deteriorating track when Sarah finally talked sense into me. Navigating around the prodigious pot holes had slowed us to a crawl. Attempting to do so at night would be the road to ruin.

At 4.20pm, with the hills either side of us bathed in the orange light of the setting sun, I reluctantly turned around. We wandered among the silhouetted joshua trees and returned to the car when the sun sank below the horizon. Mist now hovered above the ground, formed by the heat radiating off it and into the cooling air. Three months earlier, the largest collection of joshua trees in the world had stood nearby, but a wildfire had seen to that. The combination of the empty road, ground fog and charred branches made for a foreboding drive.

Soon it was too dark to see anything at all. We continued driving north-east until we arrived at the bright lights of Las Vegas.

10

LAS VEGAS

Arriving on the Las Vegas Strip felt like we'd stepped onto the red carpet at a film premiere. Bulbs flashed all around us and car horns blared as drivers, vying for space like members of the paparazzi, attempted to swap lanes in the almost stationary traffic.

To the pedants and purists among you wildly gesticulating that Las Vegas isn't in California, it's hard to disagree. Normal service will be resumed in a couple of chapters.

We had, of course, debated not coming to Las Vegas due to the pandemic. Pool parties, theatre shows and nightclubs were all closed. Most disappointingly, so too were restaurant buffets. The neon billboard towers that usually advertise restaurants and magic shows had been repurposed to promote safety measures, making it feel like we'd entered a dystopian universe. Street corners displayed slogans such as:

No Mask, No Dice
Get Your Mask On, Get Your Vegas On
House Rules...Wear A Mask

Even the replica of the Statue of Liberty outside the front of the New York, New York hotel and casino was fitted with a mask.

The ubiquity of these messages appeared to work, for the proportion of people wearing masks in Vegas was higher than anywhere else we had been in the US. When Las Vegas closed its doors to curb the spread of Covid-19 in March 2020, it was the first time the Strip had shut since President Kennedy's funeral in 1963. The pandemic crippled the city's $6.6bn gambling industry and business owners campaigned to reopen their premises almost immediately. Just 11 weeks later, state officials acceded and Las Vegas was among the first cities in the country to ease restrictions.

Upon reopening, the pressing need to fill hotel rooms contributed to a sharp fall in the price of accommodation. On my previous trip to Las Vegas, my friends and I had stayed in an insalubrious motel at the far end of the Strip behind a Hooters casino. This time, Sarah and I had a room in Paris Las Vegas, one of the best located and most recognisable hotels in the city. And it was still the cheapest accommodation of our road trip.

The website Vegas Means Business describes the hotel as "one of the most sophisticated destinations you could possibly choose for a meeting". I don't think I've ever read anything less accurate. The faux Parisian streets were fun, but undeniably kitsch. I've seen greater sophistication from a baby in a ball pit.

Directly opposite Paris Las Vegas is the Bellagio, so we crossed the Strip to watch the spectacular fountain show that runs every 15 minutes in the evenings. We huddled together against the cold desert air as we watched the jets of water dance to the sound of *Santa Baby* playing from the speakers. Our hotel's half-size replica of the Eiffel Tower was illuminated in the French colours of red, white and blue in the background, next to a two-thirds size model of the Arc de Triomphe.

To my generation, the Bellagio remains a touchstone for opulence. When it opened, it was the most expensive hotel ever built and its place was cemented in the social consciousness by the casino's starring role in the 2001 film *Ocean's Eleven*.

Sarah and I tried our luck at the cheapest blackjack table we could find inside. In a tale as old as time, Sarah and I won some money, before promptly losing it all and more. Even though the amounts we were gambling were only equivalent to a short taxi fare, I've never seen someone become as exhilarated - and then as crestfallen - by the experience as Sarah. We agreed to cut our losses. As we moved away from the table, I put my arm around her.

"It's ok. I'm disappointed too."

"I really thought we were going to win."

"I know, me too...Shall we go back outside and watch the fountains again?"

Sarah nodded despondently.

The display acted like the salve I hoped it would and, feeling more sanguine about having thrown away $30, we returned inside to admire the Christmas decorations.

Pandemic or not, Vegas knows how to put on a show and people were queuing up for the chance to get close to the biggest displays. Polars bears had been assembled from 16,500 white carnations and flamboyant red headdresses adorned 12ft tall statues of horses.

While waiting in the queue we spent time trying, and failing, to learn the rules of craps to see if we would have better luck playing that. I envisioned living out the scenes depicted in films where I stood proudly as everyone around the table cheered and congratulated my attractive wife for rolling a dice in such a way it landed on a number that made them money.

The reality was a little different. Perspex separated each section of the table to protect participants from infecting one another. Not that that was a worry on our table - no one else was there. With only a weak grasp of the rules, Sarah rolled the dice. They had to hit the back wall for the throw to be valid and to win we needed the sum of the dice to equal certain numbers. It wasn't to be and our go was over as quickly as it had begun. Another $10 well spent. At least no one other than the croupier saw it.

We'd hoped to make enough money to at least buy a celebratory round of drinks, but given our losses, we decided the drinks were now even more necessary. I opted for an overpriced bottle of beer, while Sarah, still feeling cavalier in the way all visitors do on their first night in Vegas, ordered a Bellagio Nog.

"This reminds me of Christmas at home," she smiled.

"You drink Bellagio Nog at home? You really are a high roller, aren't you?"

"No," she laughed, "but sometimes my mum would make eggnog."

"What's actually in eggnog?" I asked. As someone who doesn't eat eggs, I'd always steered clear of the drink.

"I don't know."

"So what's different about Bellagio Nog? Are we just paying for the brand name?"

"I'm not sure," she said, taking another sip. "I might need a couple more to decide."

We were sitting in a small bar elevated a little above ground level, giving us a good view of people as they entered the Bellagio. Many wore hoodies or tracksuits.

"I expected everyone to be dressed up a bit more," Sarah said.

"Unlike us, you mean," I said looking down at our jeans and trainers.

"We've only just arrived. I thought people might be more glamorous when they were going out. I brought heels and Victoria's jumpsuit with me just in case..."

"Well, don't let me stop you, but I think the Vegas you had been expecting died long before Covid."

Jeans and trainers were certainly much more appropriate for our activities the following day. We walked the length of the Strip, exploring the extraordinary attempts to replicate the canals in Venice at the Venetian, the ruins of Ancient Rome in Caesars Palace and the pyramids at Luxor. Yet in spite of the eccentric themes, the windowless casino rooms all began to look the same.

I was surprised how little the city had changed since my visit in 2012. Many of the hotels were built at the turn of the Millennium and 20 years down the line, they were beginning to lose their lustre. Las Vegas may still regard itself as the Entertainment Capital of the World, but the fact is that over the past two decades other places such as Dubai and Singapore have benefitted from major investment and are now widely perceived to be more glamorous destinations. For example, the fountains at the Bellagio were once the largest in the world, but they have since been surpassed by those outside the Burj Khalifa. Moreover, in 2007 the Chinese special administrative region of Macau replaced Vegas as the world's highest grossing gambling centre. Today, Macau's gambling revenue is nearly five times higher than that of its rival.

For years, there have been question marks over how long Las Vegas' growing population can survive in the desert. Just days prior to our arrival, the city's record-breaking 240-day streak without rain came to an end when the city was deluged by 1 millimetre of precipitation. During the following summer, Lake Mead, which was created by the construction of the Hoover Dam and supplies almost all of Las Vegas' water, fell to its lowest ever level.

In a bid to create a sustainable future, city officials identified grass as one of the worst culprits for water consumption and have pledged to remove sprinklers and turf from roundabouts and pavements. They have also handed out millions of dollars in a 'cash for grass' programme that incentivises residents to rip up their lawns. Those who don't wish to do so have been banned from using sprinklers during certain hours of the day.

As is the case in almost all of Vegas' big hotels, to reach our room we needed to walk through a casino. Regardless of whether it was night or day, people sat by the slot machines at the feet of the replica Eiffel Tower. Even in the perpetual artificial half-light, it was easy to tell many of the individuals had been there for some time.

Their faces showed neither joy nor despair. They were merely going through the motions as they put more dollar notes into the machines, scarcely noticing the waitresses who brought them complimentary drinks. Never once did they take their eyes off the scrolling symbols they hoped would land them a jackpot.

Las Vegas remains a mecca for hedonists, but you don't have to look very closely to see the city's lugubrious side. Walking across a bridge over the Strip, I saw an Elvis Presley impersonator in full white suit regalia, looking out through the metal fence. He looked as if he would rather be anywhere else in the world.

Sarah and I had enjoyed our time in Vegas, but we left the next day, ready to be captivated by nature once again. For some of the people working in the city, leaving it all behind is not so easy. For them, the phrase 'what happens in Vegas, stays in Vegas' is not so much a doctrine of silence, but a custodial sentence.

11

THE GRAND CANYON

Major John Wesley Powell was an ambitious one-armed Civil War veteran with narrow, sunken eyes and a thick beard. A geologist and former school teacher, he was determined to explore the path of the Colorado River, which ran through the last great blank spot on the map of the country.

Powell anticipated the journey would take 10 months and in 1869 he brought together a rag-tag crew of nine men for the voyage. Like him, none of them had any prior experience of white water rafting.

Many experts considered the venture to be hopeless at best and suicidal at worst. Indeed, within a month of departing one of Powell's crew, English adventurer Frank Goodman, announced, "I've had more excitement than a man deserves in a lifetime. I'm leaving."

The men's morale deteriorated as the danger increased. Rapids destroyed one of the boats and hunger set in as the food that wasn't spoiled by the river decayed in the torrential downpours of the monsoon season. Three of the remaining crew implored Powell to abort the expedition, asserting "we surely will all die if we continue on this journey." When Powell refused to countenance such an idea, they too abandoned the voyage. They believed they had a greater chance of survival walking 75 miles across the desert to civilization, than they had remaining on the boat, facing unknown hazards around every bend.

The three men were never seen again.

They are suspected to have been murdered by Native Americans or Mormons, possibly in a case of mistaken identity. Powell's expedition deputy Jack Sumner felt such guilt regarding their demise that he later castrated himself.

Just two days after the three men had walked away, the remaining crew arrived at what is today Lake Mead in Nevada. Following 98 days of hardship and misery, their nearly 1,000-mile journey was complete. They had run the Colorado River and in the process become the first recorded crew to travel through the Grand Canyon.

No one had heard from the group for three months and they were widely presumed to have died. Having survived against the odds, Powell chose to repeat the feat two years later. None of his original crew members joined him.

It was Powell who coined the name the Grand Canyon and it is in part thanks to him that the sight of the landmark's towering red craggy peaks is now so recognisable. Looking out over the canyon was undeniably impressive, yet strangely underwhelming too. The stillness of the scenery made it feel inanimate, like we were looking at a photograph.

We walked a couple of miles along the rim to try to get a better understanding of the canyon's scale. Although this helped us to put some distance between ourselves and other camera-toting tourists, it became clear that descending into the canyon was the only way to truly comprehend its size. As it was late in the afternoon, such an undertaking would have to wait, and we returned to our car to check in at a motel in the little town of Tusayan.

Recognising there were few places to stay nearby, the owners charged a small fortune for the most basic of rooms. The town itself could best be described as functional. It was epitomised by the name of the restaurant where we ate dinner, which was called We Cook Pizza and Pasta.

At the canyon rim the following morning, numerous signs warned us what a dangerous journey lay ahead. One depicted a man on all fours vomiting in the middle of the path, as if re-enacting the notorious scene in *Team America: World Police*. This seemed wildly over the top, but, judging by the fact that more than 250 people who enter the canyon require rescuing each year, apparently it's not. The chances of us succumbing to heat exhaustion seemed remote though. It was 7.45am, the ground was frozen and, if we hadn't each been wearing five layers of clothing, we would have been too.

We barely saw a soul as we wound our way ever deeper into the gorge. I'd anticipated the rocky landscape would remain largely unchanged, but its appearance altered with every 1,000ft of elevation we lost. First, sparse grasses appeared. Then hardy shrubs capable of withstanding the harsh conditions began to flourish.

We beat the sun to the lower part of the canyon. As we looked back up towards the rim, we could see the sunlight striking the Kaibab Formation at the top of the gorge, illuminating the band of yellow limestone. The canyon's famous rust-coloured rock lay underneath, and below that was the relative greenery of the flora.

A little further on was Indian Garden. Since renamed Havasupai Gardens, it's one of many names across the country that have been amended to eliminate racial prejudices of the past. Shortly before we arrived in the States, American football team the Washington Redskins lost their nickname, while the former 1960 Winter Olympic venue of Squaw Valley changed its name to Tahoe Palisades ahead of the 2021 season. The rebrand makes the resort sound like a flagship shopping centre and some skiers we met were vehemently opposed to it. But it feels like progress.

Havasupai Gardens were an oasis amongst the surrounding desert badlands and were as beautiful as they were unexpected. A doe chewed on the grass underneath cottonwood trees bursting with shades of yellow.

Visitors often underestimate the climb back up and the signs at the start had warned day-trippers not to travel beyond Indian Garden under any circumstances. It was still mid-morning though, so we took our chances and proceeded along the narrow path that led us away from the canyon wall and out onto the sunny plain.

At Plateau Point we ate lunch overlooking the rapids of the Colorado River. The canyon was formed by the river's continuous erosion of land uplifted by the movement of tectonic plates. Today, the rock at the water's edge is one mile closer to the Earth's core than that found at the rim and is estimated to be 2 billion years old.

The return journey was not as gruelling or uninteresting as we'd originally anticipated. The colours of the canyon wall looked noticeably different in the sunlight and we came across a herd of bighorn ewe, who looked at us quizzically when we ambled past.

Back at the rim, we visited the truncated stone pyramid commemorating Powell and his crews' achievements. As the sun dipped behind the canyon in the cloudless sky, the temperature rapidly dropped to zero. Most tourists hastily retreated to the sanctity of their heated cars, but we remained until it was dark. We weren't in a rush to return to the world's least imaginatively named restaurant.

12

ZION NATIONAL PARK

The only vehicles permitted in the heart of Zion are the park's single-decker shuttle buses. From where we sat at the front of the towed carriage two days later, the bus appeared to be driven autonomously, and as we gazed out of the windows at the otherworldly landscape, a recording played over the speakers. In addition to providing information about the park, the audio emphasised the importance of keeping our arms inside the vehicle at all times and the need to be wary of dangerous wildlife. We had, it seemed, arrived in *Jurassic Park*.

I didn't fancy our chances if we came across a disgruntled animal. Dressed as we were in bright red, heavy waterproof boots and waders, we couldn't outrun a tortoise. The robust shoulder-high wooden sticks we'd been given to help steady ourselves might come in handy if we were attacked, though I still didn't have much faith that Sarah's stick-beating tactics would ward off the mountain lions.

We were heading to The Narrows, an aptly named passage through a gorge. The Virgin River flows through it, so staying dry wasn't an option. And while our outfits would have been unnecessary in summer, entering the water that Christmas Day morning was a different matter entirely.

The water was only 3°C and we both sharply inhaled as we submerged our feet into the piercingly cold river. After brief calls home to share good tidings, we'd made sure we were among the first to enter the park. In many places The Narrows are less than 10 metres wide, so it wouldn't take long before the arrival of other masochists made the canyon feel congested.

Initially, the water flowed relatively slowly and only occasionally rose above our ankles as we made our way up the passage. Beforehand, I'd been sceptical the wooden sticks would be of much use, but even in the slow-moving water, they helped us to advance along the uneven riverbed. The sticks also had the unintended benefit of making us look like intrepid explorers. Or, perhaps more accurately, shepherds who had lost their sheep.

The lowest layer of rock in Zion National Park is the Kaibab Formation, the band of rock that makes up the top layer of the Grand Canyon. In Zion, the canyon consists predominantly of Navajo Sandstone, which contains remnants of the world's largest ever desert. That morning it was difficult to imagine such a landscape. Frozen sheets of ice had formed next to the waterfalls that ran down the smooth canyon walls.

As we progressed further into the gorge, sunlight began to reach the wider sections, illuminating pools of milky turquoise water and highlighting scars on the rock face, known as cross-bedding, that reveal the ancient wind patterns of the sand. Any hopes we had of warming up in the sunshine were dashed when we entered a dark, confined strait named Wall Street. As the depth of the river increased, water flowed first around our thighs, then waists and torsos. The pressure of the water displaced the air around us, creating a disconcerting suction effect that led us to briefly doubt the effectiveness of our dry bibs and overalls.

Unsurprisingly, progress was slow and was halted four miles into the canyon when a 6'7 man wearing a full body drysuit declared the section up ahead impassable. I was already carrying our extremely permeable rucksack above my head to protect our lunch and was happy to take his word for it. Sarah, who has previously held four Guinness World Records for achievements such as putting Post It notes on her body and opening champagne bottles, wasn't as easily discouraged. The water quickly rose to her armpits as she carefully placed one foot in front of the other until she'd located an underwater ledge and succeeded where the man had failed.

This being Christmas Day, protecting lunch was not a job I'd taken lightly. We'd gone all out and made a baguette with slices of turkey, salad and cranberry sauce. It wasn't roast dinner, but we were both looking forward to it.

Yet it was a resounding failure.

We were still coming to terms with the American penchant for 'everything' bread. For those unfamiliar with it, the bread is doused in a potent concoction of too many ingredients from the spice rack. It was the last time we tried it. Sarah maintains something must have gone wrong when they made this particular batch, for it tasted like it had been soaked in vinegar and dipped in onions.

It was Sarah's turn to wave the white flag. She handed me her sandwich, and while I ate my way through almost a metre of acidic bread, Sarah unwrapped a bar of chocolate. This should have been a safer bet, but she chipped one of her front teeth while biting into the frozen chocolate. Where were the After Eights when we needed them?

Sarah rolled her tongue over the newly serrated edge and I took a photo so she could assess the damage.

"I have to admit, this isn't my favourite Christmas dinner," she said, handing my phone back before sliding off the rock we were perched on. She began to stomp along the water's edge in an effort to regain feeling in her numb feet. Watching her, I couldn't help but laugh. She looked like a toddler splashing in puddles in protest at the idea of going shopping.

"Come on, let's get moving. I'm freezing!"

I swallowed the rest of the vinegar infusion and we headed back, Sarah stamping her feet all the way.

Back at the entrance to The Narrows, crowds of tourists had gathered and they looked at us in awe as they stuck their toes into the icy water. When we returned to our hotel, Sarah rushed to the shower to thaw her feet. Two minutes later when she asked me to come in, I thought it was my lucky day. Disappointingly, when she pulled back the shower curtain, she immediately pointed to her feet. They were bright purple.

"It doesn't bother me," I said, taking off my jumper.

"Seriously, my feet have never done this before. Do you think it's frostbite?"

I Googled some grim images of blackened digits before discounting the possibility. "I think you should get out, dry them and rest them on the bed. Hopefully, the colour will go back to normal once your feet have readjusted to room temperature."

Sarah raised her eyebrows. "Are you just saying that to get me out of the shower so you can jump in?"

"Pretty much."

After our lunchtime debacle, Sarah was keen to find somewhere fitting to have Christmas dinner. Predictably, almost everywhere was shut. The only exception was a restaurant which asked us to wait two hours in the freezing cold for a table. We declined and hit the supermarket

69

instead. Picking up a microwave meal seemed a bit tragic, but it turned out virtually everyone else was doing the same. The queue snaked around the aisles and we belatedly returned to our room to enjoy macaroni cheese in front of a Christmas film.

~

A decade ago, I had laser eye surgery. Many people claim to have poor eyesight, but I really did. My prescription was nearing double figures and I couldn't read in bed nor shower without my glasses.

Prior to the surgery, everyone I spoke to described the process as painless and straightforward. It was only when I felt heavy pressure on my eyeball restricting its movement and smelled the laser reshaping my cornea that I realised I'd grossly underestimated the operation.

My laissez-faire attitude had extended to thinking I could take myself home on the London Underground immediately afterwards. I'd planned to count down the stops until Stockwell, and only reconsidered when I saw the whites of my eyes were the colour of the capital's buses.

I was similarly misled about Angels Landing in Zion National Park. If the friends who had recommended the attraction had described it as one of America's deadliest hikes, I'd have been mentally prepared. Yet they failed to mention anything about the vertiginous drops that lay in store.

Before we reached them, we climbed an impressively engineered collection of 21 short switchbacks. Walter's Wiggles, as they are known, were named after the park's first superintendent, who oversaw the construction of the path in 1926.

Being a friendly chap, at the bottom of the Wiggles I said

hello to a fellow early riser as they walked along the switch-back just above me. What I hadn't considered was the fact that one minute later, we'd be crossing paths again. And again. And again. It was like when you lock eyes with an acquaintance walking towards you far up the street. Do you both look away? Or wave manically until you're side by side? By the third switchback the joke of saying "hi" was wearing thin, so we walked adjacent to one another 18 more times in silence, like two people waiting to get out of a lift to escape the awkwardness of an embarrassing gaffe.

The final half-mile of the climb was along a narrow ridge less than a metre wide in places. Chains were occasionally provided, but there were many sections without anything to protect visitors from falling 1,500ft to the valley floor.

I was amazed that in one of the most litigious countries in the world, visitors were not obliged to attach themselves to a safety cable. This is required, for example, when climbing the O2 (formerly known as the Millennium Dome) in London or Sydney Harbour Bridge. Since 2000 13 people have fallen to their deaths - including two within three months of our visit - and I'm surprised the total isn't higher.

The view from the top was incredible and our eyes followed the path of the Virgin River as it flowed through the canyon. The early morning sunshine radiated off the western canyon walls, all the way down to the green tree line at their base.

I don't usually struggle with vertigo, but my anxiety was making me twitchy. I wanted to return to safety before the impulse to throw myself over the edge developed into a compulsion. Even the simple act of taking a photograph felt like playing with fire, and I clasped my phone tightly between jittery fingers.

The journey back down was even more daunting than

the ascent. The crowds had arrived, congesting the only route to the viewpoint. It was possible to pass at only a few places and, even then, the bulging stomachs of some individuals made it a fraught process. The site attracts more than 300,000 people every year and since our visit a permit system has been introduced to limit the number of daily visitors. It's well overdue.

As someone wearing jeans at the time, I realise I don't have a leg to stand on, but I was wary of the people we saw climbing in Converse trainers. It was too easy to imagine a slip or a trip leading to a fall. Swinging backpacks also posed a threat as people turned, without a thought of the possible danger, to talk to those behind them. Rounding off this lethal combination were the children who, quite understandably, had second thoughts halfway along and insisted on retreating to safety.

Eager to get away from the haphazard queues that were now forming around the final part of the climb, we walked in the opposite direction towards the West Rim Trail. Few people venture beyond Angels Landing and we soon found the solitude we sought. Patches of thick ice and snow were common, as was to be expected in an area called Little Siberia. Around us, the dramatic rock formations were still made of sandstone, but due to the lower levels of iron oxide they contained, they were creamy white as opposed to vibrant red.

A few hours later, we were back in the main valley. We'd walked 14 miles and Sarah's feet were beginning to hurt.

"This sounds ridiculous, but I think I might have fractured some bones in my feet yesterday. I couldn't feel anything, so perhaps I didn't know the damage I was doing."

I tried to empathise, but I found it hard to believe that her stomping, however exaggerated, had caused lasting damage. So we pushed on towards Emerald Pools. Although the trail was nowhere near as high as Angels Landing, the views were still magnificent. The cottonwood trees could not have looked more different from those we'd seen in the Grand Canyon. Here, the crowns of the black, slender trunks had fine, bare silver branches with the intricacy of a dandelion head. We walked in the shade of the western canyon wall, observing the changing colours of the golden orange rock in the late afternoon sun.

That evening we ate dinner at a marvellous restaurant named Oscar's. More than two decades ago, a married couple were visiting Zion and casually told the owner if he ever wanted to sell the place, they'd buy it off him. The next day, the owner called and sold up. They've run the local institution ever since.

We'd just sat down when a woman at a neighbouring table ordered a beer.

"Sure. Can I see your ID please?" the waiter asked.

"She's got three kids," her friend laughed.

"That doesn't mean anything here," he replied. "We're in Utah."

This blunt assessment of the state's citizens, who have the highest birthrate in the country, is almost certainly unfair. Many Californians like to think of themselves as more enlightened than their compatriots in middle America, but it's worth remembering that while Utah has the same minimum age to marry as the UK, California is one of eleven states to have no minimum age at all.

As Sarah hobbled back to our room after dinner, we stopped to admire the moon. It was framed by a perfect circle, as if belonging to another galaxy. Searching online later on, I discovered the effect is called a lunar halo. It's caused by the refraction and reflection of light through ice particles suspended in wispy clouds. I also learned, much to my disappointment, that this natural phenomenon was not the once in a lifetime experience I'd considered it to be. It's actually fairly common. I had less chance of spotting a rainbow.

Satisfied that a UFO invasion wasn't imminent, we turned our attention to the cause of Sarah's foot pain. As some wise readers will have realised, her suffering was self-inflicted. Not from breaking bones on the stones in The Narrows, but by having too hot a shower when she returned. She'd developed severe chilblains.

~

Angels Landing may be more dangerous, but arguably the best view in Zion is found at Observation Point. A landslide had blocked the usual route to get there, so we drove out of the park to access a little-known alternative route. Judging by the startled look on the faces of the deer congregating on the road, few other visitors did likewise.

After descending slowly through the snow into a canyon, we reached the start of a long zigzag path chiselled out of the vertical rock face. As was to be expected at the far reaches of the park, the trail was rudimentary in comparison to Walter's Wiggles. The path was wider than at Angels Landing, but once again, the drop soon exceeded 1,000ft. I leaned heavily into the escarpment as I walked, fearing that the increasingly powerful gusts of wind would knock me off balance and over the edge.

Sarah seemed completely unperturbed. She was striding forward ahead of me, swinging her arms as if she was strolling along a beach. Near the top, she turned to see what was keeping me and was bemused to find me moving like a spider on a bathroom wall.

"Are you not a little bit scared?" I shouted over the wind.
"Of what?"

"The drop?!"

Sarah looked over the precipice, seeming to notice it for the first time. "Not really."

"There can't be many more zigzags to go?"

Sarah looked ahead. "Just three more zigs."

I paused as I took this in. "Which one is which?"

"Zigs take you to the right and zags to the left."

"I never knew that."

We set off walking again as I reflected how remiss my parents were not to teach me this crucial difference. All these years people must have felt too embarrassed to correct me.

"Of course, there's no difference between zigs and zags. That would be ridiculous!" Sarah said, feeling too guilty to maintain the pretence.

I'd like to think I'd normally be less gullible, but, distracted by the drop, I'd let my guard down.

At Observation Point we were 700ft above Angels Landing and could look down beyond it along the length of Zion Canyon. We sat down to eat our remaining turkey, now sandwiched between plain bread.

As we did so, I couldn't help but overhear the conversation between the only other people nearby. An old man stood in an ill-fitting leather jacket next to his diminutive younger Asian American girlfriend.

"Linda, this is beautiful isn't it?"

"Yes, it's nice."

"We've been together for a long time, haven't we?"

"Yes, more than three years."

"Linda, will you marry me?"

"Ah." She paused. "I guess so."

"You guess so?"

"Well, I like you."

It was the most underwhelming proposal I ever hope to

witness. I desperately wanted to disappear into the red dust at my feet. It's not as if my own proposal had been flawless. After a lengthy preamble in which I struggled to get the words out, I went down on one knee in a nettle-infested sheep wash in Lyme Regis in Dorset on the south coast of England. Sarah's tears of joy at least befitted the occasion.

By the time we finished our picnic, the weather had closed in and the view of the rock formations at the opposite end of the canyon had been obscured by snow swirling in the distance. No longer able to bend the fingers in our gloved hands, we beat a hasty retreat. I was pleased we'd zigged and zagged halfway down the canyon walls before the snow reached us.

13

DEATH VALLEY

We were ready for some warmth, so it was convenient that our next destination was both the hottest place on Earth and the driest in North America. Given this, it was quite a surprise to be approaching Death Valley in the midst of one of the most intense storms we'd ever seen. The Pontiac's poor windscreen wipers could barely keep up. In a region that receives only 20 days of precipitation a year, we appeared to have hit an unsolicited jackpot.

The rain had stopped when we arrived, but dark clouds remained above Golden Canyon. This was the filming location for *Star Wars: Episode IV - A New Hope*, where R2-D2 was zapped by Jawas. Walking between the tall, close canyon walls either side of us, it was easy to recall the scene. At least it was for me. Sarah feigned interest.

From Zabriskie Point we looked across the labyrinth of heavily eroded, yellow mudstone ridges to the valley's sweeping salt flats, before hiking back through Gower Gulch. Neither of us had heard of the word 'gulch' before travelling to the States, but it appears frequently on US maps. For those as equally unaware of the geological term as us, a gulch is a deep V-shaped valley that has been formed by river erosion.

Human intervention has caused Gower Gulch to become a misnomer and it has long since lost its V-shape. Instead it resembles a giant upturned staple, its dry 100ft wide riverbed lined by banks 20ft tall. In an area prone to rare but dangerous flash floods, this alteration was an inevitable consequence of the decision in the 1940s to redirect water in such a way that the gulch's drainage basin increased by more than 16,000%.

We returned to the car under an inflamed pink sky. It was as if the setting sun was capitalising on the rare appearance of clouds to showcase its brilliance before darkness fell.

The little accommodation that exists in Death Valley was out of our price range, so for the duration of our time at the national park we stayed in the small nearby town of Beatty. It's the kind of place most people would only stop at to buy petrol, but it's home to one of the most unforgettable communities we came across in America.

Our motel consisted of a row of ground floor rooms that ran parallel to the road through the town. A naked bulb hung from the ceiling and a small portable heater stood by the bed. After wryly observing the light dim when we switched the heater on, we went out to find somewhere to eat.

All eyes were on us as we pushed open the wooden saloon doors. A sign reminded customers to wear a mask inside, but no one was.

Two men in their fifties with unkempt grey hair perched on bar stools by the till, ready to engage with anyone buying a drink. They were seeking conversation rather than free booze, but the alternative would have been preferable. Regardless of how clearly we spoke, they pretended they couldn't understand anything we said while wearing masks.

After Sarah had repeated the word "England" for the third time, one of the men said, "Ah, just take the mask off. There isn't any Covid in Beatty. I doubt there ever will be. It's just a story to sell papers."

He paused to have a slug of beer. His attitude was reminiscent of the Soviet Union's response to the AIDS crisis in the 1980s, when up until 1987 the official line was that it was impossible for a Russian to have HIV.

"What's it like in England at the moment?" asked the man next to him, who had been nodding in agreement with everything his friend had said.

"It's quite bad," replied Sarah. Considering at this point most of the world had shut its borders to Britain to try to prevent the spread of the 'UK variant', it was clear he hadn't been following much of the coverage.

"Are you sure you're British?" the other man chipped in. "You don't look British. You're too tall."

This flummoxed us. I was under the impression that British people were considered to be tall. Not as much as the Dutch, but at 5'10 and 6'2, Sarah and I have rarely felt like giants. Perhaps he was looking for a reason to discredit Sarah's summary of the situation in the UK. We assured him our accents were real and the barmaid - who had no problem understanding us - served us our drinks. She very kindly put them on the house, for which we gave her a sizeable tip.

The tipping culture in America causes anxiety for many first-time visitors and it took several weeks before I didn't panic when faced with the 18.5% default minimum tip on the electronic display menus. Did my reluctance to pay this when I was picking up a pastry at a bakery counter make me a terrible person? Or just British?

Initially, we were even confused about *how* to tip. When you pay by card in bars and restaurants in America, you tip by writing a number down on the receipt before you walk off. This is de rigueur, yet it feels susceptible to abuse. Unscrupulous businesses could add $1 extra onto every customer's tip without getting caught for years.

I couldn't blame anyone but myself for some accidental underhand mathematics when we went out with Ashwin, one of Sarah's fellow Fellows, for dinner one night. Sarah routinely shirked tipping responsibility and it was once again left to me to handle our end of the transaction. When I should have divided the bill into thirds and paid two-thirds, I mistakenly paid for only half the cost of the total meal. Seeking to rectify this, I offered to cover the tip. The only problem was I wrote it on Ashwin's receipt. Poor guy. It was the most expensive biryani he'd ever had.

In the bar, a scraggly old man with a heavily bandaged hand was telling anyone who would listen that he knew all about rocks and there was a rich vein of mineral resources running under his property. He emphasised that he didn't want to sell up, but when he did, boy would he be rich. Wary of catching his eye, we busied ourselves studying the walls of the bar, which were covered in paraphernalia. This included out of state registration plates, car parts and fake dollar notes defaced with scribbled annotations such as 'Lava Girls 08'.

When a mother and daughter entered the bar, the man approached them to tell his improbable tale. They listened patiently until the end, but much to his disappointment, instead of asking about his subterranean riches, they were more interested to learn what had happened to his hand.

"I busted it fallin' off the chair over there on Christmas Eve," he said.

Two men on our right were having a similarly farcical

conversation. Except there wasn't anything funny about this one. I couldn't work out whether it was the premise I found most disturbing, or the measured, philosophical tones in which the subject was dissected. The discussion surrounded who were the "good black men". Their moronic list, for what it's worth, extended to the following: Morgan Freeman, Denzel Washington, Jesse Jackson and James Earl Jones (the man who voiced Darth Vader in *Star Wars*). According to these bigots, not one famous good black man has been born since 1955.

The next morning we drove back into the national park. The road stretched more than 30 miles across a wide plain towards, and then through, the snow-covered Amargosa mountain range and for much of the drive we could see the empty tarmac running in an uninterrupted straight line ahead of us.

Astonished to see snow in the last place we expected to find it, when we reached the mountains Sarah suggested we walk to one of the lower summits. Unwilling to be seen to blink in the face of her spontaneity, I pulled over.

Conveniently, the person who'd come up with the plan was wearing hiking boots. Not anticipating such an adventure, I was wearing old trainers with worn down tread better suited to moonwalking. From the car, the ascent had looked manageable and neither of us had fully appreciated the difficulty of the climb. There wasn't a path to the top and I slipped repeatedly traversing the icy scree. Shielding my eyes from the glare of the morning sun, I fell further and further behind Sarah until her salmon pink jacket was just a dot on the hillside.

The sparse tufts of grass were soon covered by snow and

the only visible vegetation were short, resilient red cacti. Their attractive spiky hearts would have looked more at home in the *Little Shop of Horrors* than among this blanket of ice.

From the peak we traced the road all the way from Beatty to the floor of Death Valley far below. Miles into the distance, we could see other snowy apexes rising above the plateaus. I'd imagined Death Valley to be a vast, flat expanse, but its topographical range is one of the largest in the United States. These mountains play a significant role in generating the park's record-breaking temperatures, as they trap the heat radiating off the ground.

The hottest ever temperature on Earth had been measured in the valley just four months earlier. A fact that might have been better received if Sarah wasn't shivering from having waited so long for me to catch up.

Few visitors see Death Valley from this standpoint and even fewer see it covered in snow. There hasn't been measurable snowfall on the valley floor for almost a century, but we subsequently learned that snow is found most years on some of the surrounding mountains. So the occurrence wasn't quite the historic event we'd believed it to be. Nevertheless, the map showed we'd reached an altitude comfortably in excess of 5,000ft. Which wasn't bad for an impromptu early morning pit stop.

We returned to the car and resumed our day in the more customary fashion of visitors to Death Valley. Due to the distance between the park's attractions, and the extreme heat of the summer, Death Valley is not the kind of place you can explore by foot. Rather, it's more like a shopping list, where you drive from place to place, ticking off items in a procession.

The first stop was the Devil's Golf Course, where large,

rough salt crystals extended for miles into the distance. Unfortunately, their interest couldn't live up to the landmark's name, so we didn't stay long before visiting Badwater Basin. Death Valley's most famous site owes its name to the high salinity of the spring water, which makes the little water available undrinkable. Unlike at Devil's Golf Course, the salt crystals at Badwater Basin formed fascinating, tiny white towers.

Thousands of which were crushed every minute under tourists' feet.

Averting my eyes from the destruction, I looked up towards a sign on the rock face which marks the sea level. Here, at the lowest point in North America, it was nearly 300ft above us.

After a quick break for lunch, we began a nine-mile scenic drive to Artists Palette. This was a drive thru of nature, for those whose interest in geology was usually reserved to fossil fuels. We joined the stream of traffic observing the effects of oxidation, which had caused the rocks on this part of the Black Mountains to turn shades of red, green, yellow and purple.

Our final stop was a hike into Mosaic Canyon. The drive there took almost an hour, but encompassed only a fraction of the valley. The canyon's name is derived from a rock formation composed of a mix of colourful, angular rocks stuck together in a natural cement. It's widely complimented, but for me it brought to mind the 1970s fashion for crazy paving. I much preferred the canyon's polished marble walls and the golden light cast by the late afternoon sun along the lip of the canyon.

Shortly after entering the gorge, the walls became narrower and it became necessary to scramble up, over and around rocks. Most hikers turned back when the route reached a 20ft high slanted rock face, but we pushed on until we finally called it a day at the bottom of an impassable 30ft dryfall.

The walk had started at the end of a long dirt track. Navigating the pot holes in the dark as we drove back was far from easy and we were grateful for the light of the full moon. We suspected the astronomers donning head torches in the car park were not so appreciative.

Due to the lack of options in Beatty, we returned that evening to the bar we had visited the night before. Attempting to avoid the two men who, once again, were sitting by the till, Sarah discovered a dining room out the back which contained a shuffleboard. For those new to the game, this is played on a 22ft table where competitors attempt to accurately slide four weights to the opposite end of the table. It's effectively a miniature version of curling. Minus the ice and the brooms.

Unlike Sarah, I'd played before, but as is often the case, she quickly gained the upper hand. A single traveller in his twenties watched us for a while before talking to us at length about his recent travels to Eastern Europe. When he left, the chef seized his opportunity.

"That boy needs to get a hobby. He was in here yesterday too, pestering people."

"Oh, it's fine - it's nice to meet a fellow traveller," Sarah said.

"Normally, we'd have a much bigger crowd of tourists, but Covid's seen to that."

"I can imagine."

"It's all the politicians' fault of course." I nodded in agreement, assuming he was referring to the muddled approaches adopted by world leaders in response to the pandemic. "You see, they're forcing doctors to fabricate the numbers," he said.

I stopped nodding.

"Statistically, 99.98% of people survive Covid. It doesn't fit the narrative, but far more people die of tuberculosis each year. Did you know that?"

I shook my head.

"We've known TB's infectious for more than a hundred years. Have we lived in fear ever since? No. You know over 460,000 people die in this country every year from TB?"

"No," I said, surprised. "Is it really that many?"

"Yep. The fact you didn't know shows how much the media is hiding." He paused as he ran his fingers through his thinning hair. "I don't believe in conspiracy theories, but this thing, whatever it is, must have been created in a lab. We don't know why yet. What I do know is that I'm not buying any of this stuff about it being created by mixing with bats. That's bullshit."

I bit my lip and moved my head noncommittally. As soon as he'd uttered the phrase "I don't believe in conspiracy theories, but...", my faith in the credibility of his argument had eroded faster than Gower Gulch during a flash flood. Satisfied he'd made his point, he returned to the kitchen to wash up. I hadn't wished to labour the point as I didn't have any evidence to hand, but I was highly sceptical that more than nine times the number of Americans were dying annually of tuberculosis than had died throughout the whole of the Vietnam War.

You won't be surprised to know they're not.

Approximately 9,000 Americans die of tuberculosis each year (compared to 350 in the UK). This figure is tragically high, but in light of the pandemic, the absence of these deaths from the headlines appeared somewhat short of a cover-up.

In the days that followed, I reflected on the erroneous and alarming conversations I'd witnessed over the past two nights. Was my failure to challenge these individuals a sign of apathy, resignation or just cowardice? I wouldn't have ignored such comments if a friend or relative had made them. My only justification was that I knew my words would do little to change the opinions of those articulating them. Not that they would have heard them underneath my mask.

14

LAKE TAHOE

We'd hoped to make Lake Tahoe the final destination of our winter road trip, but finding an affordable place to stay over the festive period had proved impossible. So rather than seeing in the New Year in a private chalet, we were spending it 45 minutes away beside unheralded Lake Washoe, at the home of a couple in their sixties.

It might have been at the wrong lake, but the large house featured an outdoor hot tub and an expansive garden looking out onto the mountains. Inside, a heavily decorated Christmas tree stood in the corner of the open-plan living room and small red stockings hung off the mantlepiece.

Our hosts were a funny couple. They both loved outdoor pursuits and enjoyed their ritual of starting every morning with a game of backgammon. But that was where the similarities ended. Eddie was garrulous, while Edwina was direct, and whereas he was tall and thickset, she was petite. Yet the most striking contrast was in their political outlooks. Eddie was a Democrat while Edwina was an avowed Republican. Eddie made an effort to wear a mask in the kitchen during our stay, but Edwina bore no truck with it.

When we asked if they wanted us to wear masks, she

said, "Do what you like, no one is going to make me wear a mask in my own house."

The topic was clearly a bone of contention between the couple and Eddie brought the subject up again over dinner.

"So, Sarah, let me ask you, as a scientist, what do you think about wearing masks?"

"Err...well, I'm an engineer, not a scientist, but...I think it must help."

"You see Edwina? It's not just me."

"She just said she's not a scientist!"

"But you're a doctor, right?"

"Yes. Although not that type of doctor."

"But you work in a hospital?"

"Yes."

Eddie raised his eyebrows ever so slightly, like a defence barrister unveiling the evidence of their best witness.

"At Stanford?"

"Ye–"

"Eddie," Edwina interjected, "you're not going to change my opinion on this, stop trying!"

I half expected Eddie to look at me and say "no further questions, m'lord". Disappointingly, he didn't and we instead all sat in awkward silence, desperately thinking of a way to change the subject.

A fresh dusting of snow fell overnight. The road conditions worsened as we drove towards the trailhead in the mountains the next morning, but Sarah's driving was as delicate as her diplomacy the night before. Unlike the roads, the car park at our destination hadn't been cleared of snow for some time though.

"I reckon park up over there," I said, pointing to a corner

of the car park sheltered by a large tree. "It won't be as deep there."

Sarah put the car into reverse, but it wouldn't budge.

"I think we're stuck."

"Just give it a bit more vroom."

Sarah did so. The car sank.

I cursed. We both started looking for cardboard or anything flat we could place under the tyres. As my eyes skirted around the car, I realised the cause of our problem. The handbrake was on.

Both so alert to the perils of driving in the snow, we'd failed to spot the obvious. With the handbrake off, and a nudge from me, we were soon moving again and able to laugh about it as we put on the snowshoes we'd borrowed from Eddie and Edwina. They resembled fat, shortened skis fitted with crampons under the sole of the foot binding. Having never used snowshoes before, we were excited to try them out. The only problem was working out where to go. The path was submerged under nearly 2ft of snow and it was clear that no one had walked the route for some time.

After a few wrong turns following notches in the trees that turned out to be just animal scratches, we made it out of the woods and onto a steep, exposed ridge overlooking Lake Tahoe. The blanket of grey cloud we had driven through that morning had disappeared and the intricate perfection of the snow-covered pine needles shone against the vibrant blue horizon. Snowflakes fell miraculously from the empty sky as we gazed out at the lake and beyond to the peaks on the western shoreline.

We'd set out intending to reach Marlette Lake, but time was against us and we never made it that far. It felt inevitable that we would lose our way on the loop back and far from certain we'd be able to find the path again in the dark. Initially steadfast in her determination to continue, eventually Sarah relented and we headed back through the trees towards the car.

En route, we descended a steep hill and I enjoyed the sensation of allowing my feet to catch my fall, just as I had in the Mojave Desert. Much to Sarah's amusement, my jeans, rucksack and hair were soon covered in snow. My poor shoesnowing technique caused the snow to flick up behind me as I started each stride, making it look like I was on a treadmill in a snow globe. I was having so much fun I didn't care.

That was until icy water began running down my back.

Armed with a greater understanding of the conditions, the next day we made less ambitious plans and bought a toboggan. Or we would have done, given a bigger budget. Instead, we made do with a bright orange $15 plastic saucer. The slope was filled with the squeals of excitable children sledging and we were, by a distance, the oldest people there without offspring.

At the only vacant space on the brow of the hill, I dropped the saucer to the ground. By tucking my knees tightly to my chest, I could just about fit inside, and, with the aid of a gentle push from Sarah, I was on my way.

Sledges, it turns out, are like bin bags and toilet paper. You get what you pay for. Aboard our bargain basement purchase, it wasn't possible to keep facing the same direction, never mind steer. As I accelerated downhill, I was spun more times than a giant teacup at a fairground.

Halfway down the slope, I discovered why no one else had been sledging here. A large, partially submerged pointed rock lay directly in my path. I desperately tried to navigate around it to little avail and was unceremoniously ejected from the saucer when it glanced off the side of the rock.

Grinning ruefully, I walked back to the top and handed the sledge to Sarah.

"What happened?"

"There's a hidden rock where I fell off," I said through heavy breaths. "You'll be fine. Try to choose a side to go past and you should avoid hitting it. Just don't crash into one of the children instead." I gave the saucer a push to send her on her way. "Good luck."

Sarah hit the rock with a force that caused the saucer to briefly become airborne before crashing into the snow. Her tailbone collided precisely with the tip of the rock and when I reached her she was bent over in pain. After just one aborted run, Sarah was forced to retire. So too was the sledge itself, which had ruptured along its radius.

Nearly everyone has hurt their tailbone at one point or another and knows the agony of doing so. To sufferers, it seems almost unfair that the injury doesn't show any external indication of the pain. When Sarah undressed a few days later, I did something I never normally do. I recoiled. There was a large brown smear around the top of her bottom. I'd never seen anything like it, and admittedly, my initial thought was she'd forgotten how to wipe. But the bruise, quite literally, highlighted the extent of Sarah's injury.

Sarah wasn't able to sit down for days and we needed to borrow a pillow and place every unused jumper we had on the passenger seat to make car journeys tolerable. Considering her head touched the roof of the car, other drivers must have assumed she was 7ft tall. Or auditioning for a part in *The Princess and the Pea*.

Sarah is nothing if not resilient though. Others would have retreated to their accommodation immediately after the accident, but Sarah merely suggested moving on to the next item on the day's itinerary.

So we strapped the snowshoes on and headed to Chick-adee Ridge. During our ill-fated trip to the toboggan shop, we'd been given various types of bird seed and encouraged to try our luck at feeding the birds. Having scouted out the most comfortable fallen log she could find, Sarah sprinkled some seeds into her palm. She then held it out expectantly at shoulder height, like a waitress carrying an imaginary plate.

"There's no way that's going to work," I scoffed. "We need to go somewhere where we can at least hear birds. We're not in a Disney fil–"

At that instant a bird landed on her hand and collected some seeds in its beak.

We were both startled. Shocked by the fact the event she'd hoped would happen had actually occurred, Sarah jumped, causing the bird to take flight. My cynicism was replaced by envy and I held out a hand of seeds to see if I too could have my *Snow White* moment.

We waited in silent anticipation with our hands raised parallel to the sky. To anyone unaware of this local tradition, we'd have looked absurd. Fortunately, the bird soon came back for more and word quickly spread of our generosity. The birds visited us one at a time, as if they had formed a queue high up in the trees. All were chickadees, which look much like monochrome blue tits. Lake Tahoe lay in the distance below us, but for once, our attention was elsewhere as we tried not to react to the ticklish sensation of the little claws resting on our palms.

It didn't take long for us to start bickering over who the chickadees liked more.

"I think they prefer me."

"You just have bigger hands."

"And longer arms," I added, extending my arm towards the sky.

I neglected to mention that I'd weighted the competition in my favour. No one was nearby, but judging by how picky the chickadees were in regard to which of the seeds they ate, they weren't worried about going hungry. They reminded me of buffet goers who insist on only eating smoked salmon. By judiciously selecting some of their favourites, I ensured Sarah was left with the aviary equivalent of dehy-drated cucumbers and limp lettuce.

She didn't stand a chance.

15

A NEW HOME FOR THE NEW YEAR

On our return to Palo Alto, we moved into an annexed studio that was even smaller than our previous place. So small it featured in the UK's biggest national newspaper. At the bottom of the article, readers commented "This is grim" and "That looks awful". One asked whether we were renting the property or whether it was simply the location of where we were "being held hostage indefinitely". Not bad for a place that cost us $1,800 per month.

Our new neighbourhood was three miles from the centre of town, but just a few minutes' walk from two Hollywood legends. We regularly visited Perry, the 26-year-old miniature donkey who was the model for the character of Donkey in *Shrek*. Judging by the way he chewed the edge of my hoodie, he was as big a fan of me as I was of him.

The other nearby star of the silver screen was Shirley Temple, the 1930s child star rumoured at the peak of her career to be a 30-year-old dwarf. Like Lenin, when she died nine years ago her body was placed in a mausoleum, which we visited in the cemetery opposite our studio.

We don't usually delve into the macabre, but Sarah and I had also recently visited the Stanford Mausoleum on the university campus, where the Stanford family were laid to rest.

Leland Stanford's broad shoulders and sturdy physique had helped him to cut an imposing figure in Gold Rush California. His success as an industrialist saw him accrue wealth and influence and in 1862 he was elected State Governor at the age of just 38.

After 18 years of marriage, his wife Jane gave birth to their only child shortly before her 40th birthday. Tragically, Leland Stanford Jr died when he was just 15 years old, having contracted typhoid in Athens while the family were on a Grand Tour of Europe.

Seeking a way to commemorate their son's life, the Stanfords began purchasing land to build a university. Initially, Leland Stanford Sr proposed building it in Mayfield, a neighbouring town to Palo Alto. His one condition was that it banned alcohol. Mayfield was the location of several rowdy saloons and the town's residents baulked at the request, so the Stanfords established a new, dry, town in Palo Alto.

Stanford University began accepting students in 1891 and Palo Alto grew rapidly as academics moved to the town and built houses in a neighbourhood still known as Professorville.

Leland Stanford Sr died of heart failure in 1893, leaving Jane to secure the university's long-term future. She funded the institution almost single-handedly for 12 years, until she died from poisoning. Her murder remains unsolved.

By this point the die had been cast and Palo Alto annexed Mayfield 20 years later. *The Mayfield News* wrote its own obituary, declaring, "We have watched Mayfield grow from a small hamlet, when Palo Alto was nothing more than a hayfield..."

16

BODEGA BAY

Apart from Christmas, public holidays in winter are an alien concept to British people. Yet more than half of US federal holidays fall between November and the end of February. One reason for this could be the fact that as American workers receive such little corporate holiday entitlement, these days help to tide employees over until the summer months. Or simply that the chances of a national holiday being a total washout is far smaller in the US than in the UK, so there isn't the need to schedule public holidays for the warmer months. Nonetheless, it was surprising that while the UK has two days of Bank Holiday to mark Easter weekend, the comparatively less secular US population has none.

Martin Luther King Day falls just 10 business days after the Christmas break and we took the opportunity to visit Tomales Point at Point Reyes. Located less than 50 miles north of San Francisco, the area is famous for its coastal views and for the wild elk that roam there. The only obstacle to enjoying both is the weather. Point Reyes is the second foggiest place in North America.

The clear blue sky over the Golden Gate Bridge was an

encouraging sign, but, true to form, an impenetrable thick grey mist descended as we arrived at our destination. In other circumstances we'd have been impressed by the rapid transformation. One minute we were worried we hadn't brought enough sun cream, the next we were driving through a cloud.

Almost as inescapable as the fog was the litany of roads and geographic landmarks named in honour of Sir Francis Drake. He is believed to have landed at Point Reyes in 1579, midway through his global circumnavigation. He remained there for five weeks, while the expedition crew made repairs to their ship, the legendary *Golden Hinde*. During this time, the crew had many friendly interactions with the Native American Coast Miwok, who no doubt wouldn't have been quite so welcoming if they had known that Drake had claimed the area for Queen Elizabeth I and renamed it Nova Albion.

The mist never once threatened to lift as we walked along the ridge to the end of the peninsula. We spotted the outlines of some elk in the distance, but it was not until the very end that we saw the waves crashing onto the beaches. Point Reyes had, we reluctantly admitted, lived up to its reputation.

We drove onwards to Bodega Bay, where Alfred Hitchcock's film *The Birds* was set. As we were staying in the town, we felt obliged to watch the film. I've previously jumped out of my skin watching Harry Potter, so I usually avoid horror movies at all costs. Sarah promised to hold my hand if I became scared, but as it turned out, I needn't have worried. *The Birds* doesn't hold up particularly well.

Obviously, animation has advanced considerably over the 60 years since the film was made. Hitchcock famously used real birds to attack actress Tippi Hedren, but for much of the film, the mechanical birds looked more comical than threatening. Moreover, the number of questionable decisions made by the characters undermined the tension. Why, for example, if you were concerned the birds may attack, would you force all the schoolchildren to go outside?

Sarah's favourite animals are goats, so once she'd learned there was a room available in Bodega on a goat farm, there was only one place we were staying. It felt more like Yorkshire than California as we drove through the green fields of the countryside. The region is renowned for its cheese, and the following morning Sarah was keen to participate in some pastoral farming by feeding the goats.

While she did so, my head was turned by the arrival of Annie, the farmer's huge Anatolian shepherd dog. Her broad, golden shoulders nudged up against my thigh as she greeted me. Despite her age, she continued to dutifully tolerate the cold each night, patrolling the farm's borders and keeping the coyotes at bay. According to her owner, she could still appear ferocious when necessary, but judging by her laboured movement, she relied entirely on the deterrent of her bulk and her bark. She enjoyed the attention we gave her and when she saw us driving down towards the farm's entrance, she quite intentionally blocked our path by lying down in the middle of the narrow gravel drive. Picking her up wasn't an option and it took a lot of coaxing for me to get her back on her feet to clear the path. Prior to arriving at some Airbnbs we worried about the prospect of being snowed in, but we'd never considered the risk of being trapped by the unconditional love of a giant dog.

Belatedly, we began a hike near Bodega Head. The fog of the previous day had disappeared, replaced by record-breaking hot weather. We had anticipated experiencing more winter sun in America than we received in the UK, but even our fellow Californians were surprised by 25°C temperatures in early January.

A British summer can go by in the blink of an eye, but each spring the first spell of warm weather is imbued with a feeling of optimism. The nation replaces its jumpers and jeans with summer dresses and shorts and looks forward to the promise of long summer days ahead.

In sun-drenched places such as California, winters aren't as protracted, nor as difficult to endure, so it's understandable citizens are not quite as deliriously grateful when hot weather returns. Yet the unexpected burst of warmth that arrived in California that weekend generated something close. Young families strolled around the headland, eating lollies from ice cream vans and smiling as they watched a man create bubbles the size of astronaut helmets. Each one slowly mutated as it floated over the cliff edge in the temperate sea breeze.

Almost everyone had driven here, but they had missed out on some of the best parts of the peninsula. Our route had taken us across empty sand dunes covered in wild grasses and colourful ice plants. Amid the carpet of vivid green, yellow and red fleshy fingers, the first of these succulents had begun to bloom, dotting the landscape with bright pink and yellow flowers. The plants' existence is not to be celebrated though. They belong to an invasive species whose thick mat of vegetation chokes the life out of its native competitors. I was similarly ignorant about the prevalence of imported eucalyptus trees in California. Their existence sparked memories of their native Australia, but the oil they contain, and their propensity to shed bark, hinder efforts to bring wildfires under control.

After watching seals congregate on an island off the cape, we returned along the beach, where we were entertained by crowds of tiny sanderlings. The birds feed on invertebrates buried within the upper intertidal zone. For this reason, they stood as close to the water's edge as they dared. Every time it looked like their feet might get wet, they fled across the sand. Each new wave spurred their legs into a flurry of motion as they scurried diagonally up shore to outrun the gently lapping waves.

The next day we returned to Point Reyes National Seashore. In the sunshine, the landscape was unrecognisable from its appearance two days earlier. Not only could we now see the tip of Tomales Point, more than 10 miles away, but even the Farallon Islands, 20 miles off the coast. Today the islands are closed to the public, but they were visited by Drake's crew, who hunted for seal meat in preparation for the journey across the Pacific that would take them back to Plymouth.

Before we too returned home, we walked on the beach at Limantour Spit. As we sauntered along the shore, we spotted a large grey object about 80 metres in front of us in the middle of the otherwise featureless sand.

"What's that? A rock?"

Sarah squinted. "It looks like a dead whale."

"Eurgh. I think we'd have smelt it by now if it was."

When a putrid rotting whale corpse washed up on a beach in Oregon in 1970, local authorities turned to dynamite to dispose of it. The council hoped the whale would be blown up into pieces that would then be eaten by seagulls. But even after the explosion, much of the whale remained intact. The detonation only succeeded in attracting news coverage, now available on YouTube, of an event that left residents running for their lives as falling chunks of whale blubber destroyed parked cars.

We approached slowly until we were 10 metres away from the mystery obstacle.

"Well, it's not a whale," I said, advancing in a wide arc away from the animal's face. "But it is enormous."

The mammal was comfortably the largest sea creature

I'd ever seen out of the water. It was almost 12ft long and could have devoured Anatolian shepherd dog Annie in just a few mouthfuls.

"Is it alive?" Sarah asked.

We both watched, stock still, as we looked for signs of life. Through all the blubber we couldn't tell if it was breathing.

I was relieved when the animal eventually blinked. The bomb squad could stand down - he was merely sunbathing. Although aware of our presence, he didn't seem perturbed. Two years previously, Sarah and I had watched seal pups playing on a beach in Norfolk. The mammal before us looked like a seal, but of a completely different order to anything we'd seen then.

"Is it a walrus?" Sarah suggested.

"I can't see any tusks, but maybe that's because his face is buried in the sand. Can you get it to smile?"

"I think it was you he was winking at."

Neither of us could think of another animal he might be, so agreed we'd chalk it up as a walrus. It turns out that was doing this monster of the sea a disservice. He was far larger than a walrus. Subsequent research revealed he was a northern elephant seal weighing approximately two tonnes. I'm glad I didn't try to persuade him to move out of the way.

17

MONTEREY AND CARMEL

Four weeks later we drove nearly two hours south to Monterey for Presidents' Day weekend. The coastal town is famously located next to picturesque 17-Mile Drive and the white sand beaches and illustrious golf courses that line the route frequently see it referenced as one of the world's greatest drives.

But anyone seeing it from the seat of a car is doing it wrong.

We had decided to rent bicycles even before we learned that by doing so we would avoid the $11 entrance fee. The store owner insisted we couldn't so much as touch the bikes until we had signed a lengthy contract promising not to sue if we were injured. Our request to borrow helmets was met begrudgingly though. It seemed he couldn't care less about the risk of head injuries - so long as he wasn't liable.

San Diego is the only city in California older than Monterey, but the latter's regional significance has greatly diminished since the 19th century. At one stage it was the only port of entry for all taxable goods into the state, but the city's streets are now full of tourists rather than traders. People crammed onto the pier at Old Fisherman's

Wharf, where social distancing was sacrificed on the altar of their mutual desire to receive the regional communion of seafood chowder served in sourdough bread bowls. It was early in the day, but soggy chunks of bread were already beginning to accumulate in the bins like coconut husks.

We cycled on to Cannery Row, a waterfront street renamed in honour of John Steinbeck's novel of the same name. In the opening sentence of the book, Steinbeck described the street as "a poem, a stink, a grating noise, a quality of light, a tone, a habit, a nostalgia, a dream." It's difficult to think of a less fitting description for the street today. The smell, dirt and characters of Steinbeck's time were a consequence of the sardine canneries, which disappeared in the 1950s as a result of overfishing. Standing in their place are tourist shops and overpriced restaurants.

After passing the city aquarium, we stopped at Lovers Point Park. Chubby ground squirrels foraged for edible detritus among the sea defences, while countless canoodling couples did their utmost to ignore the cold wind blowing off the Pacific.

We ate lunch on Asilomar State Beach, just around the corner from the oldest continuously operating lighthouse on the west coast of the US. Looking beyond the young children running in and out of the waves, I saw something move. Several pieces of wood floated on the surface of the churning sea, so it was only when the object moved out of sight, and then immediately reappeared a couple of metres to the right, that my scepticism disappeared.

It was a sea otter.

Soon we could count a handful bobbing up and down as they dived between the waves. When they weren't lying on their backs on the surface eating clams, they resembled hoax photographs of the Loch Ness monster, their distant head and shoulders exposed as they scanned their surroundings.

I kept a lookout for otters as we cycled around the headland, jubilantly pointing them out as if they were yellow cars. 17-Mile Drive doesn't just provide opportunities to spot local wildlife though. It also provides a glimpse of the lifestyles of the super-rich. That evening we looked up some of the properties for sale that we passed. The old adage that money doesn't buy taste still rings true. You could spend tens of millions of dollars to buy one of these exclusive mansions, yet still have to spend a fortune eradicating the gaudy interior design of some of the properties. Furthermore, the queues of nosey tourists driving along the residential streets would, we suspected, quickly dull the thrill of living in such a prestigious neighbourhood.

Of course, some of the houses up for sale in the area were sensational. Nevertheless, our favourite US real estate advert belonged to a far more modest property 300 miles north on Tolowa Trail road. The listing attempted to whip up potential interest by asserting [capitalisation original] "TALLY IT UP, TAKE A LOOK, TOLOWA TRAIL IS OFF THE HOOK!". There are many house buying practices in the US we hope never to see in the UK, such as the exorbitant agents' fees and the expectation prospective buyers should write sycophantic 'love letters' to the outgoing property owner in order to curry favour. However, the use of cheerleader chants is certainly one we'd welcome.

The proximity of the properties along 17-Mile Drive to Pebble Beach golf course is regarded as a perk, but it has its disadvantages. Play impedes the homeowners' privacy and leaves them vulnerable to wayward shots. One might argue that players who have stumped up $615 for the privilege of teeing off on the world-class course are good enough to know where they are hitting, but the fact that more than

50,000 balls have recently been recovered from the seabed suggests otherwise.

Few of those belonged to the players participating in the golf tournament under way that day. We hadn't realised it, but we were cycling through the grounds while some of the world's best players were competing. We must have looked incongruous on our rental bikes next to the wealthy spectators and hardcore fans.

We stopped for a short break in the seaside town of Carmel. Located on the southern shoulder of the headland, the town's affluent residents are both figuratively, and literally, well-heeled. This is because local legislation prohibits individuals from wearing heels more than two inches high.

The law was introduced to protect the council from liability in the event someone tripped on a tree root emerging between cracks in the pavement. Much like the owner of the rental bikes, the council's concern doesn't appear to extend beyond covering its back though, for it has never installed street lights in the town.

Carmel is notable for a number of other strange quirks. One such peculiarity is that there are no street addresses. Properties are instead identified in the wider context of their location. For example, a fictitious home address could be written as San Benedict, 5 SE of 14th. This would mean it was on San Benedict Street, five homes south-east of 14th Avenue. Pity the poor couriers who have to interpret this.

For several decades eating ice cream was banned too, on the grounds that it would make the streets sticky. Fans of gelato were calling out for a hero and found it in the shape of Hollywood actor Clint Eastwood. A man after my own heart, when he was elected mayor of the town in 1986, he immediately repealed the anachronistic law.

Sadly, we didn't have time to take advantage of this amendment before we set off to complete the less scenic loop back to Monterey. Upon returning the bikes, Sarah suggested we share a 24-inch takeaway pizza for dinner as a Valentine's Day treat. At first I was affronted by the assumption we'd share it, but after being unable to get the box through the restaurant's front door without putting it on its side, even I was willing to split it.

And people say romance is dead.

A few weekends later we ventured further south along the coast on a camping trip to Big Sur. At the beginning of the 19th century the area was considered as difficult to access as anywhere in the country and was often impassable in winter. This all changed with the construction of California State Route 1.

No longer a remote backwater, the region now attracts as many visitors as Yosemite National Park. In the 1950s, the American writer Henry Miller asserted "Big Sur is the California that men dreamed of years ago...the face of the earth as the Creator intended it to look." Pioneer conservationist John Muir would likely have argued Yosemite was equally befitting of such a description, and it's certainly the case that the national park is easier to pinpoint on the map. Big Sur's lack of defined boundaries is a legacy of its past, when Spanish settlers referred to the isolated area south of Monterey as 'el pais grande del sur' (the big country of the south).

After spending a day hiking in Andrew Molera and Julia Pfeiffer Burns state parks, the next morning we headed 15 miles down the coast to McWay Falls. The landmark was the cover image of our *Lonely Planet* California guidebook and was named by *Condé Nast Traveler* as the Golden State's most beautiful place. So it was unfortunate we didn't manage to see it. Thick fog had rolled in from the ocean, obscuring our view of the waterfall, which is one of only two in California that falls directly into the sea. We had better luck at Alamere Falls, north of San Francisco, where the other 'tide-fall' cascades into the Pacific.

In an attempt to brush off our disappointment, Sarah suggested we pull into a cafe on our way back. Unbeknownst to us, we'd stumbled upon one of Big Sur's most popular drinking spots. From the cafe's sunny hillside terrace we looked down in awe as the pure white mist moved over the ocean and converged halfway up the mountainside. Big Sur may not be as inaccessible as it once was, but on days such as these it must look much the same as it did to early European explorers. The first of these, Juan Cabrillo, wrote that the landscape was filled with "mountains which seem to reach the heavens".

Stopping for an impromptu drink at a fancy cafe felt indulgent, but it turns out we were in good company. The cafe was previously a house belonging to Orson Welles and Rita Hayworth, who bought the property on an impulse when driving through Big Sur in 1944. They never stayed a night there. Decadence is a sliding scale, I guess.

The next stop was Garrapata State Park. As there isn't a car park, most drivers are oblivious to its attractions and speed past as they head north. But those fortunate enough to find space in a layby can access one of the most spectacular places on the coast. The Santa Lucia mountain range, which boasts the steepest coastal slope in the contiguous US, runs through the park. Once clear of the fog, it wasn't long before we were drenched in sweat.

One false summit followed another as we hiked through woodland and then along meandering paths bordered by tall bushes full of lilac flowers. I'd proposed the walk as a short pit stop and it seemed most visitors had similar intentions. Upon seeing what lay in store, many turned back and we soon had the scenery to ourselves. Its beauty was all the more impressive given that most of the park was destroyed in 2016 by what was, at the time, the most expensive wildfire to control in US history.

Our only company came in the form of stripy brown western fence lizards basking in the sunshine. Like teenage boys in a gym aware that a girl is about to walk by, they started doing press ups as we approached. They do this to attract females and intimidate rival males. We weren't sure whether the performance was for Sarah's benefit or mine, but just as is the case with posturing adolescent boys, the effect of their endeavours was comic rather than compelling.

At the peak it looked like we could walk straight off the narrow, dusty path and onto an impenetrable quilt of white clouds. As they retreated, we caught sightings of the rocky islands 2,000ft below us. State Route 1 also became visible. We followed the road with our eyes as it snaked along the coastline and traced our route home.

18

PINNACLES NATIONAL PARK

It's a tale reminiscent of the Hugh Grant film, *The Englishman Who Walked Up A Hill And Came Down A Mountain*: a community comes together to persuade officials to upgrade the status of a local landmark. Yet whereas in the film Welsh villagers were hauling soil to convince cartographers, in real life Californians were cajoling Congressmen.

In some respects their campaign to re-categorise the Pinnacles as a national park, rather than a national monument, was just as arbitrary, but they too ultimately succeeded. The Pinnacles' new status was signed into law by President Obama in 2013 and the area remains California's newest national park.

At the end of April, we drove 100 miles south-east of Palo Alto to see if the area deserved the honour.

While putting up the tent, I waved down a man driving a buggy connected to a trailer full of firewood. I wasn't sure the wood was for sale and his gruff demeanour suggested I was about to get an earful for stepping out in front of him. But his face lit up when he heard my English accent. It seemed that in spite of the Pinnacles' upgraded status, it hadn't yet become a fixture on the international tourist trail.

Americans' appreciation for British accents may be a well-worn stereotype, but it still holds true. During our time in the country, many people told us how intelligent it made us sound. I did my best to put them at ease with my nonsensical musings, but these efforts were immediately undermined when conversation turned to Sarah's career. People loved our British idioms and thought it was hilarious when I asked if I could "chuck a mug in the dishwasher". Cultural exchanges are a two-way street though. I was just as amused hearing the American pronunciation of buoy (boo-ee).

The only thing many Americans enjoyed more than our British accents was the opportunity to regale us with their stories. The man with the firewood was no different.

"When the campsite was shut down last year, one army officer - can't remember his rank, but he was pretty senior - had just arrived with his family. They'd sold their house and intended to spend six months camping across the country. When the shelter in place order kicked in, they didn't have anywhere to go. He knew he'd be decommissioned if he ignored the ruling, so he was given special dispensation to stay here for the duration. We kept the toilets open and just made them use bleach." He scratched his unshaven jaw. "'Course, that ruined the septic tank, so that needed to be replaced. Still, there are worse places to be stuck than having all this to yourself."

"Definitely," I agreed, trying not to imagine the state the pit toilets must have been in.

"Over time, I got to know the guy. Would you believe, he went to Yale *and* Stanford University?" the man said with a shake of his head.

The concept seemed so outlandish to him that he regarded it as more remarkable than the pandemic itself, which he brushed off as an inconvenience. My own academic record wouldn't have merited comment, but I knew

Sarah's would have given him a thrill. We were too British to mention it, and the opportunity to be an anecdote shared with future campers passed us by. Leave no trace, as they say.

Before lighting the newly purchased firewood we walked around the campground and admired our fellow campers' shiny silver Airstream trailers. Each resembled a miniature zeppelin tethered to an SUV. Large black birds spiralled high above us and we strained our eyes attempting to convince ourselves we were observing the park's famed condors. They were most likely just turkey vultures.

Almost as common as turkey vultures were acorn wood-peckers. The sound of their beaks knocking on bark was a regular soundtrack to our weekends away. Their distinctive red hats and black and white bodies made them easy to spot and it was amazing to watch them fly at speed, retracting their wings at the last possible moment to disappear into the perfectly circular miniature holes in the trees where they nested. Some of the drivers on California's roads were evidently not as skilled, judging by the smashed glass and detached car wing mirrors that lay scattered by the toll barriers.

The campsite was home to fluffles of rabbits. Such groups are also known as colonies, but referring to them as fluffles seems far more fitting. While walking up the hill next to our tent we spotted a long, stripy black and brown snake with a noticeably wider brown stripe on the end of its tail. We kept our distance and hoped the rabbits did likewise.

Returning to our campsite, we cooked burgers, sausages and corn on the cob. All of which wouldn't have been half as tasty if we hadn't managed to acquire the firewood. Blue flames flickered across the charred logs, illuminating them like a city viewed at night from a plane. I was enjoying the sound of the cicadas and the crackle of the burning wood when I heard a scratching noise a few metres behind us.

After staring into the fire, my eyes struggled to adjust to the surrounding darkness and I walked unsteadily towards the location of the noise. When I reached the picnic table, I jumped back. A large raccoon had climbed on top and was feverishly trying to open the rucksack containing our food. My involuntary shriek startled it and the raccoon fled empty-handed.

Sarah couldn't stop laughing. "I had a feeling it might be a raccoon. I saw a sign by the toilets."

"You didn't think to tell me?"

"I thought I'd let you investigate. Anyway, what would you have done? Armed yourself?"

"I dunno, maybe. He was much bigger than I'd imagined. I doubt my spork would have been much use."

The following morning we walked among the park's rocky spires. A consequence of lava flow and millions of years of weathering and erosion, these pinnacles have created a playground for climbers. Hiking through the verdant canyons felt like walking across the palm of a giant hand, its ashy red fingers emerging from the ground around us and pointing to the sky.

We were strolling side-by-side along a narrow path when I heard the sound of maracas close by. I realised instinctively there was only one possible explanation. I looked down and saw with horror that less than 20cm away from the toes of my sandalled left foot was a rattlesnake.

For the second time in little more than 12 hours, adrenaline coursed through me. I recoiled and let out a cry of terror, which raised in pitch like a singer practising scales at double speed. While Sarah had been able to guess and react accordingly to the cause of my consternation the night before, she had no idea what had prompted a similar reaction this time. She decided she wasn't going to hang around to find out and ran forwards, inadvertently putting the rattlesnake between us.

Fortunately, the snake was not aggressive and the shake of its tail had seemingly served as a warning of its presence, rather than an indication of its intention to strike. While I summoned up the courage to walk past it at a marginally safer distance, the snake decided it had better places to be and slithered off into the bushes.

A few minutes later, Sarah and I were discussing what our contrasting responses revealed about our character, when we saw another, less recognisable snake. This prompted me to look back at the video I'd recorded of the snake the night before. It was, we realised, a rattlesnake. That 'wider brown stripe on the end of its tail' wasn't, it turned out, a stripe at all.

We carried on walking uphill around the towering rock formations until we came to a staircase carved in stone. Wide enough only to walk in single file, the route wrapped around an enormous boulder. Just before the normal dusty trail resumed, the path gently descended and I came across a lean man in his fifties walking briskly towards me.

"Move out of the way," he said in a thick French accent.

"I can't, sorry," I said. "There isn't any space. If you just go back three metres, we can let you pass?"

"No. I'm going uphill so you have to move."

"It stays this narrow for the next 60 metres or so - you can't expect me to go all the way back?"

"You have to. It's my right of way."

"What?" I said, confused as to why he was making this such a big deal. "That's not how it works. Just go back three metres and then there is plenty of space."

"No."

"Well I'm not going back."

By this point Sarah had caught up and could see the exchange had deviated dramatically from the nodded exchanges we usually shared with hikers.

"If you'd just moved back, you would already have passed us by now," I said.

"It's for *you* to move," he persisted, and restarted walking towards me. At a time when many hikers were still putting on face masks every time they passed within five metres of each other, I now had one close enough to kiss.

"This is ridiculous," I muttered, as I climbed onto a nearby rock. Sarah did the same and the man strode, full of righteous indignation, underneath us. I consoled myself with the thought of how he might fare adopting a similar attitude at Angels Landing.

The likelihood of glorious weather makes camping a far easier and more appealing prospect in California than in the UK. However, camping in the UK has at least one advantage. In America we relied on a cool bag to prevent our food spoiling in the heat. This by and large worked, but could be found wanting on the final day of a long weekend away. So when I saw Sarah tucking into a bowl of cereal the next morning, I was relieved and followed suit.

"Eurgh! That's rancid!" I said, as soon as I put the spoon in my mouth.

"Is it?"

"Yes!"

"I thought it tasted a bit funny, but I didn't want to say anything in case it put you off."

"It would have done."

"I just didn't want to prejudice your opinion."

"Well thanks. You didn't even bat an eyelid, though? I've no idea how that milk hasn't curdled."

Sarah looked despondently at her half-eaten breakfast. "Do you want the rest of mine?"

"No!"

My mum has previously worked as a 'supertaster' testing new products before they go to market. It's an enviable gig, but one only available to individuals whose taste buds pass the stringent vetting process. Sarah's would not cut the mustard.

Her palate might not be up to par, but Sarah's stomach has the constitution of a coyote. Our contrasting experiences during a trip to southern India were a testament to that. So I wasn't worried the soured milk would provoke an adverse reaction. The cumulative effect of several weekend hiking trips had though exacerbated a long-standing knee injury, which put paid to our plans to go on another walk.

Instead we spent the day at Seacliff Beach. This, we discovered, is home to the concrete ship SS Palo Alto. Commissioned during World War I in response to concerns about impending steel shortages, the ship was completed too late to be deployed. It was mothballed for several years before it was intentionally grounded at the end of Seacliff Pier to serve as a casino and a dancefloor. The owners went bankrupt during the Great Depression and the ship's subsequent deterioration is such that we first mistook it for a collapsed section of the pier.

Regrettably, no one thought to remove the oil before the ship was grounded. In 2003 the tanks on the forgotten ship cracked, spilling fuel and killing hundreds of birds. The clean-up cost an estimated $1.7m, approximately the same as the ship cost to construct.

19

YOSEMITE

It's not common practice to adopt highways in the UK, but businesses of all sorts get in on the act in America. Two of my favourites were 'Bridgeport Gin Club' and 'Flyhi', a cannabis delivery service. Both would appear to undermine the impact of roadside warnings such as 'Don't let drunk or high drive'. Either way, it can't help that the command reads like it was written by someone under the influence.

Some of the highways were even sponsored by citizens. The possible motives for this are unclear, but you know someone's panicked when you open a Christmas present to find you've adopted a highway.

On the way back from Yosemite National Park, the following four organisations had adopted roads in close proximity to each other:

Sikhs of Tracey
Sikhs of Mountain House
Union of Sikhs
League of Sikhs

We drove along this route on several occasions and each

time the rattling of the fittings inside the Pontiac briefly subsided as we travelled across the smooth surface of the newly laid tarmac. This established an unhelpful connection in my mind between road building and the Sikh community. I worry it may one day land me in hot water.

Yosemite is one of the crown jewels of the national park system. It contains approximately 3,200 lakes and more than one-fifth of California's 7,000 plant species. In 1864 part of Yosemite became the first tract of land to be set aside by the US government for preservation and public use, creating a precedent for the creation of Yellowstone as the country's first national park eight years later.

We wanted to camp in Yosemite, so we waited until May to visit the park. Our camping experiences in America varied considerably. At one extreme was a glamping trip for my birthday, where we had garden games, heaters and a large double bed. At the other, was a night spent in a stranger's back garden. We were asked to stay away from the house, which wasn't ideal when we found the toilet roll we'd been issued had blown off the open air potty into a puddle.

Camping is more popular than ever in the US and in 2020 more than 10 million people went camping for the first time. Considering the stunning landscapes America has to offer, it begs the question what took them so long.

This newfound appetite to explore the great outdoors should be celebrated, but it required trips to be planned six months in advance to secure a campsite. It felt like I was back in the UK, trying to buy reasonably priced train tickets.

In a year when borders were shut, nowhere was higher in demand than Yosemite. A campsite reservation in the national park was the equivalent of a golden ticket. Despite manically hitting the refresh button when the tickets were released, we missed out and instead stayed in Curry Village. The 'resort', which has been operational in the park since the 19th century, still consists primarily of very basic tents. Sadly, prices have risen from the $2 charged back then, to $160 per night.

This doesn't include access to a firepit, so Sarah and I soon found ourselves joining the queue of people at a pizzeria in the park. The line tailed all the way back to the visitor centre, where small televisions mounted on the wall played dated videos of bears entering vehicles containing food. The videos, which served to remind visitors that cars are damaged every year by hungry bears, were unintentionally hilarious. As they approached each car, the bears glanced guiltily left and right, like a toddler eyeing up a freshly baked chocolate cake. They'd then squeeze their large frames through half-open car windows. If they couldn't, they would smash their way in. Once inside, they often sat in the front seats, eating the food as if they were at a drive-in cinema.

The sunset turned Half Dome's iconic face a luminous gold as we ate our pizzas. Except for those at either end of the age spectrum, everyone was transfixed. The children, gleefully chasing each other around the old wooden storage huts, remained oblivious to the spectacle, while the grizzled old-timers were too busy regaling anyone who would listen with memories of the park from the '70s to notice. If you believed their wistful nostalgia, back then it had hardly changed since Ansel Adams' day.

The sun hadn't yet reached the valley floor when we headed out at 8am the next morning into the cool air. To test Sarah's knee, we started the weekend gently by wandering along Tenaya Creek to Mirror Lake. As one of the most accessible hiking destinations in the park, the small beach around the lake is often crowded. However, most visitors only come to see the perfect reflection of Mount Watkins in the water and don't venture beyond it.

Initially, we passed lush, empty grassland, but it wasn't long before the riverbank was lined by woodland. Above the trees, Yosemite's grey monoliths loomed large, but by mid-morning even their great peaks couldn't prevent the sunlight from illuminating the trail.

We stopped by one of the several clear, chartreuse pools of slow-moving water and looked at the partially submerged tree trunks beached in the river following months of near record-breaking drought. I inhaled sharply as we dipped our legs into the freshly melted snow water and within minutes my numbed legs had turned red in silent protest. Mindful of the cryogenic benefits, I distracted myself by watching the butterflies landing next to us. Each of their delicate white wings was embroidered like linen.

Underwhelmed but unsurprised by her lily-livered husband, Sarah was undeterred by the cold and was itching to go for a swim. When we found a sand bar further along the path, she needed no further invitation. Peer pressure forced me in too.

We returned to the historic Ahwahnee Hotel for a drink. Queen Elizabeth II and numerous US presidents are among the guests to have stayed in the accommodation during its 96-year existence. I didn't spot any VIPs during our visit, and it was hard to avoid the suspicion that many of the individuals sitting nearby had little inclination to explore the scenery beyond the windows of the wood and stone structure.

Sarah and I tried to channel this sentiment as we nursed our drinks and read books on the lawn. We'd set our sights on completing an ambitious 19-mile hike called the Yosemite Grand Tour the next day and we'd promised ourselves we'd take it easy until then.

But we were impatient to discover the landscape around us and set off to see Yosemite Falls. Consisting principally of two distinct drops, Yosemite Creek cascades almost 2,500ft to the valley floor, making the waterfall the tallest in continental North America.

Adjacent to Yosemite Falls, in the centre of the valley, is the park's famous meadow. Walking on the elevated boardwalk across it in the early evening spring sunshine, it was easy to imagine how irresistible the long grass must have been to the sheep who lived here 150 years ago. The presence of the livestock contributes to a bucolic image, but their impact was devastating. By the 1890s the sheep had decimated this hugely diverse habitat and grazing was belatedly banned.

Having suffered no ill effects from the day's adventures, we began finalising our plans for the following day. The Yosemite Grand Tour combines four popular routes in the park into one greatest hits album featuring the valley's biggest attractions.

We found the route on the AllTrails app we relied upon for many of our walks in the States. To our surprise, some of our favourite hikes received one-star reviews. This was often because the reviewer noted the presence of poison oak. A threat we were oblivious to before we crossed the Atlantic, it appears poison oak is the only thing that scares American hikers more than mountain lions. Sometimes fellow walkers would barely step aside to let us pass in case they brushed up against the plant. It was many months before we learned to identify the species, which frequently produces sets of three leaves in shades of red and green. We regularly heard parents reminding their children to stay away, using the dictum, "Leaves of three, let them be". This might be why we saw so many clovers.

We managed to avoid touching poison oak for more than a year. Throughout that time we doubted it was much worse than a stinging nettle: highly unpleasant and best avoided. But hardly meriting dire warnings in a land filled with deadly wildlife.

Our complacency did not go unpunished.

When Sarah's face came into contact with the plant, it became blotchy and swollen. We're still not sure how it happened, but for a few days she looked like the kind of middle-aged woman who shares a house with nine cats and a dismembered ex-husband in the freezer. In hindsight I should have kept this observation to myself. It was just as well we only had a small freezer.

The Yosemite Grand Tour remains the greatest single-day walk Sarah and I have ever completed. Having hiked nearly 150 trails covering 1,200 miles across California, we don't say that lightly. But perhaps it was only to be expected as the national park has quite the back catalogue. Nevertheless, one recent review states:

★☆☆☆☆
Do not for any reason go on this trail…I almost fell off a cliff.

Many other reviews focused not on the stunning terrain, but on the route's total distance.

Even though AllTrails users are, by nature, lovers of the outdoors, it would appear the platform harbours as many keyboard warriors as any other online community. Some people insinuated other hikers were idiots or liars for having the temerity to suggest the route was a different distance than was calculated by their own GPS gadget. It goes to show, you could give people $1m and they'd still complain it wasn't in their preferred denomination.

The first part of the route was along the Mist Trail. The name is derived from the spray that drenches hikers as they walk next to Vernal Fall. May, it turns out, is an excellent time to explore Yosemite as hikers benefit not only from warmer temperatures, but are also able to witness the national park's waterfalls in full flow. Photographs taken just a few months later are practically unrecognisable and are a sad reminder of California's dwindling water supply. We paused to admire the rainbows created by the sunlight in the mist, before walking two miles further east to Nevada Fall. A narrow wooden bridge spanned the top of the waterfall, under which the Merced River roared towards the edge of the precipice.

We continued ascending along a section of the 200-mile-long John Muir Trail. Shortly after diverting from the well-known route, we stumbled upon one of the most beautiful and rarely seen views in Yosemite. Looking down to where we had just stood, we could see the water gushing through the granite bottleneck at the top of Nevada Fall and watch it plunge towards the sloped rock face below. Next to it was Liberty Cap, a 7,000ft peak that towers above the waterfall like a giant upturned thumb.

Pleased to have finally reached a plateau, we walked west and soon spotted Yosemite Falls on the other side of the valley. Just around the corner on our side was Illilouette Fall. A powerful, dramatic waterfall nearly 400ft tall, on any other hike Illilouette Fall would be the standout landmark, yet in a geological playground such as Yosemite, it's relegated to almost a footnote.

After pausing briefly by the waterfall, we started climbing again towards Glacier Point. We ate lunch nearby, tracking our journey by counting the waterfalls we could see that we'd passed along the way. Directly opposite us, the Merced River flowed down Nevada Fall towards Vernal Fall, on a route aptly described as the Giant Staircase. To the south-east we could see Illilouette Fall and to the north-east, was the unmistakable side profile of Half Dome.

Glacier Point must be one of the best viewpoints in the world. In addition to the sights already mentioned, it provides an excellent view of Yosemite Falls. But we didn't stay long. Our arrival coincided with the reopening of the road to the viewpoint for the first time that year and the area was overrun with tourists.

Oh to have the good fortune to enjoy the majestic views with only the few individuals who had hiked to the summit.

We escaped the crowds and began the imaginatively named Four Mile Trail. The final leg of the Grand Tour saw us return to the valley floor via a succession of switchbacks. I'd anticipated this section would be relatively low-key in comparison to what had preceded it, but the location high above the heart of Yosemite granted us superb views overlooking the pine forest and the vertiginous grey walls either side of it. Our calves were burning by the time we returned to Curry Village, where we celebrated our achievement with another well-deserved pizza.

Reluctantly, we headed home the next day. Before we left we visited El Capitan, the location of the nerve-shredding Oscar-winning documentary *Free Solo*. When we approached the bottom of the intimidating rock face, we both gingerly climbed a few feet off the ground. I had hoped visiting this climbing mecca might inspire me, but clinging to the rock, my discomfort merely underlined that I was a rank amateur in the footholds of legends.

I would enjoy reading reviews on AllTrails of the climb up El Capitan. It wouldn't surprise me if someone had written:

★☆☆☆☆
No ropes provided. Watch out for the poison oak at the start.

20

THE AMERICAN DREAM

By early June the course at Stanford was wrapping up. All that remained was a presentation to the great and the good of Silicon Valley's medical technology community, in which Sarah and her colleagues would summarise their findings.

As this was a virtual event, I had no excuse for not attending. I just couldn't bring myself to. I'd heard Sarah rehearse her speech from the other side of the table so many times, I felt I could have delivered it myself. Even if I still struggled to comprehend what half of the acronyms meant. The MedTech sector (thankfully at least this contraction is relatively straightforward) must be one of the few industries that can rival cryptocurrency for the sheer number of baffling abbreviations. I never stood a chance of understanding the difference between a HIFU, a CVC and an ECMO. Lacking a PhD, all I was left with was FUD (fear, uncertainty and doubt).

Enough misunderstandings occur without using acronyms. At one point, Sarah tried to arrange a meeting with a clinician who said she couldn't attend because she was in the hospital. Sarah replied that this wasn't a problem, as she was working in the hospital herself that day. It was only then that the clinician clarified she was in the hospital because she'd been admitted. The exchange reminded me of a tweet I'd recently read from writer @samuel_pollen:

> European out-of-offices: "I'm away camping for the summer. Email again in September."

> American out-of-offices: "I have left the office for two hours to undergo kidney surgery but you can reach me on my cell anytime."

The tweet went viral because it satirised a fundamental truth. Broadly speaking, there seem to be two types of people in California. Those who take every opportunity to explore the state's incredibly varied landscapes, and those who seldom switch off from work. The latter's reluctance to disconnect has its roots in the fallacy at the heart of the American Dream.

The myth that anyone can make it if they work hard enough has led people to believe you must sacrifice everything to rise to the top. You should be available at all times of the day, and ideally make yourself completely indispensable.

To these individuals, their dedication becomes a matter of personal pride. They don't think twice about interrupting their beach or skiing holidays to participate in unessential business meetings. I recognised this kind of behaviour from my time working in cryptocurrency, where the global community of opportunistic traders and startup founders frequently uttered the mantra "crypto never sleeps". By contrast, Sarah's unwillingness to check her emails while on holiday marked her out not only as European, but downright odd.

Such attitudes may be particularly prevalent in the

startup hotbed of Silicon Valley, but they're replicated across North America. According to a Gallup survey published in 2021, US and Canadian workforces saw the highest levels of stress of any region in the world, with 57% of workers feeling stressed daily. This is considerably higher than the 39% of employees who feel this way in Western Europe.

If working yourself towards an early grave in the pursuit of professional success is an enduring American tradition, so too are elaborate graduation ceremonies. In front yards across the neighbourhood, placards endorsing Biden for president were gradually being replaced by good wishes for the local high school students of the class of '21. The disappearance of the political posters may have reflected Biden's falling approval ratings, but it also represented a show of support towards a demographic deprived by the pandemic of their chance to live out the storylines of hundreds of Hollywood movies.

The graduation ceremony organised for Sarah's course was scaled back compared to previous years, but I still arrived feeling like I'd turned up at a wedding. Rows of white seats had been set out in preparation across the garden lawn, all facing a vine-covered pergola. And just like at a wedding, I knew only a fraction of the people there.

In the run-up to the event, Sarah and her colleagues were tasked with delivering a 'roast'. This was an opportunity for them to poke fun at their course directors. Sarah's growing anxiety about the group's reluctance to rehearse only increased my levels of anticipation. It promised to be an exquisitely excruciating watch.

I should have known better.

Given that none of the Fellows wanted to damage their relationships with their well-connected teachers, mentors and lecturers, the roast was decidedly lukewarm, featuring gags that were as gentle as they were niche. *Saturday Night Live* it was not.

21

FOG CITY

The end of Sarah's course and the expiration of our tenancy fortuitously coincided with Steve and Lucy returning to the UK on holiday. In exchange for watering their basil plant, they generously offered to let us stay at their flat. Thrilled to have the opportunity to stay somewhere with more than one room, we jumped at the chance.

Locals often play down the extent of the fog in San Francisco, but the 'Fog City' nickname seemed justified to us. The timing of our arrival in mid-June may have been unfortunate, but from our hilltop accommodation, much of the time it felt like we were living in a cloud. Invariably, as soon as we left the city, the sky would magically clear. Perhaps it's because we're starved of sunshine in Britain, but it seemed it would be a shame to live long-term in one of the few places in the Golden State that doesn't receive daily doses of Californian sun. Certainly, it felt as if we were a lot further than 35 miles away from Palo Alto, where we'd been wearing shorts for months.

Judging by the surge of gentrification in the city over recent years, many people don't share our reservations. Uber, Airbnb and Salesforce are just a few of the companies to have their headquarters in San Francisco and their collective growth has caused the demographics of some of the city's neighbourhoods to change significantly over recent years. A report published shortly before our arrival in the US found that San Francisco and nearby Oakland experienced the highest rate of gentrification between 2013 and 2017 of anywhere in the country, with high wage earners replacing families with low household incomes in nearly one-third of neighbourhoods. This affluence is never clearer than on a weekend morning, when the streets are lined with people queuing outside bakeries for more than 30 minutes to buy coffee and pastries. They don't come cheap. Danish-style rye bread at local favourite Tartine costs almost $15 a loaf.

One of the neighbourhoods trying hardest to resist gentrification is Haight-Ashbury. The area rose to fame in the 1960s as a focal point of the flourishing hippie movement and the streets are still lined with colourful street art, counterculture book shops, craft stores and tattoo parlours. Conveniently, it was also the location of our nearest supermarket. Strolling downhill every Monday, I marvelled at the novelty of being able to complete the humdrum task of the weekly shop in the centre of a community steeped in cultural heritage. Arguably it's not much different from going shopping in Camden in north London, but everything feels more exciting when you're abroad.

Bolinas, a coastal town located 20 miles north-west of San Francisco, is one of the few places that comes close to matching Haight-Ashbury's anti-establishment credentials. Haight-Ashbury rapidly declined following the Summer of Love in 1967, and the rise of violent drug crime led many residents to relocate to Bolinas, where they sought to create a liberal, peaceful paradise that could become a haven from capitalist greed.

The town is notoriously difficult to find as residents have for years torn down local road signs in an effort to reduce the number of visitors. Undeterred, one weekend we stayed the night. The ramshackle appearance of some of the buildings and the town's relaxed atmosphere suggests that more than half a century on, the ethos of Haight-Ashbury's hippies endures. Judging by a conversation we overheard while eating fish and chips on the beach, free love does too. At least for some.

"Honey, I'm sorry but you knew you were marrying a player." The man's grey ponytail swayed from side to side as he spoke loudly into his phone. "This was always a possibility."

Astonished by his brazen tone, I turned to Sarah. "What are the chances of you taking me back if I ever used that line on you?"

"None. I wouldn't have picked up the phone," she replied.

The mix of people from all walks of life makes San Francisco a fascinating place to people watch. One of the prime locations to do so is from a corner of Mission Dolores Park referred to as Gay Beach due to its popularity with the LGBTQ+ community. From its steep banks, the view stretches out across the open parkland towards the skyscrapers of the financial district. On sunny weekends, thousands of people flock to the park and you can see yummy mummies chatting with friends, tech millionaires walking pampered dogs and gay men in tight speedos sunbathing alone or drinking with friends. All while speculating how many tan lines the goths' outfits will leave them with at the end of the day.

Four blocks away is the Castro. It was one of the first gay neighbourhoods in the US and remains at the forefront of global LGBTQ+ activism. The area's 'anything goes' spirit is well-known, but I was still taken aback when halfway through dinner a naked man strutted past. Victoria was seated beside me, and, having lived in the city for several months, she wasn't anywhere near as surprised.

She simply raised her eyebrows and said, "You haven't been to the Castro unless you see a penis."

On another weekend Sarah and I visited a bar with live music. We hadn't been sitting down on one of the outdoor benches for long when the man next to us struck up conversation.

"So are you here for the band or just for Pride?"

The answer was neither, but it seemed an easier white lie to suggest the latter. I was soon grateful for that decision, as our newfound friend turned out to be a superfan who would have rumbled my pretence within seconds. Eager to tell us what we'd been missing all these years, he talked us through the relative merits of previous albums and the location of the band's upcoming gigs.

When we left him to enjoy the second half of the performance 40 minutes later, I turned to Sarah. "Did you know it was Pride week?"

"No. I'm glad you didn't let on though. We'd have looked like philistines."

In our defence, because of the pandemic the city's famous Pride Parade had been cancelled. En route to the bar we'd seen several men dressed in figure-hugging black leather and had passed other men carrying purses decorated as pigs. However, we'd assumed it was typical San Francisco. We were simply pleased they were clothed.

Liberalism may now be di rigueur in San Francisco, but the city hasn't always been so open-minded. San Francisco's immigration office on Angel Island opened in 1910 and quickly gained a reputation for racial discrimination. The island's location in San Francisco Bay drew comparisons with Ellis Island in New York, but whereas immigrants were often welcomed to the Big Apple, arrivals to Angel Island were ostracised. Over the course of 30 years, administrators on Angel Island processed the applications of almost 1 million immigrants to the west coast of America. Nearly a fifth of these were rejected. In New York, where the proportion of Asian immigrants was far smaller, only 2% of applicants were refused. Upon arriving at Angel Island, Chinese and Japanese immigrants faced intense questioning and thousands were detained for many months. One individual described how officials had "locked us up like criminals in compartments like the cages at the zoo".

Today, almost 200,000 people travel to Angel Island each year. This sounds like a lot, but is only a fraction of the nearly 1.5 million people that visit nearby Alcatraz. Angel Island is 35 times larger and, in contrast to the bleak appearance of its more illustrious neighbour, much of it is covered in woodland.

From the island's summit we could look around in all directions and see the Golden Gate Bridge, the marina at upmarket Sausalito and the silhouette of the city's skyscrapers three miles away. While walking around the perimeter of the island, we paused at the abandoned buildings of Fort McDowell military base to watch the mule deer roam freely among the encroaching yellow spring flowers. Unsurprisingly, the Angel Island mole, which is not found anywhere else in the world, wasn't as easy to spot.

Over the years, the island was equipped with various weapons to act as a last line of defence to protect the citizens of San Francisco. In the 1950s 12 Nike anti-aircraft missiles were placed underground, ready to thwart a potential nuclear attack by the Soviet Union. Large notches were cut into the hillside so the radar system could communicate with the launch site, but within eight years the missiles were obsolete.

Realising we were running out of time, we hurried back to catch the last ferry of the day. I was confident the authorities wouldn't want tourists to be stranded on the island and assumed the ferry would remain at the jetty for a short time to pick up stragglers.

I was wrong.

The crew lifted the gangway behind us and the boat departed as scheduled. We were especially pleased to be aboard when we learned it would have cost $200 to charter a private water taxi back to San Francisco.

For all the city's myriad attractions, our stay coincided with my one and only bout of homesickness. Euro 2020 was to blame. Although not technically a home tournament, every England match but one was played at Wembley Stadium. Home tournaments don't come around often, and good performances by the national team are even rarer. I remembered being gripped by Euro '96 and revelling in the collective joy generated by the London 2012 Olympics, so I knew what I was missing as England progressed to the final. I watched one game in a pub, but found it too painful having to listen to the opinions of those around me. As a result, I watched the other matches in the apartment, battling my phone's poor internet connection to see history be rewritten a few pixels at a time.

I tried to sate my passion by buying tickets to a local sports fixture. After watching England narrowly beat Denmark in the semi-finals, Sarah and I travelled to Oracle

Park, the home of baseball team the San Francisco Giants. It was my turn to be the ignorant spectator. We marked ourselves out as such by making the foolish mistake of turning up for the start of the game. Many fans hadn't yet made it into the ground and the few who had were more interested in buying hot dogs. It feels sacrilegious to say, but the fans' ambivalence to catching the start is understandable. The Giants play at least 162 games per season, with each game usually lasting more than three hours. Even when they were seated, following the action appeared secondary for many 'spectators'. It simply represented a better place than home to hang out with friends.

The 42,000-seat capacity stadium is built on the waterfront. On the east stand we ambled along the walkway between the pitch and the Pacific, looking at the ferries docked at the neighbouring piers and watching the players perform under the prematurely illuminated floodlights. A scoreboard records the all-time number of home runs where the ball lands in the water. Such 'splash hits' are rare, but I suspect are more common than the number of times a football is kicked into the Thames from Fulham's similarly located Craven Cottage stadium.

Public transport is better in San Francisco than in other American cities, but that's a pretty low bar. We knew the journey back across town would be convoluted and slow, so after watching the Giants claim victory over the St Louis Cardinals, we opted to try one of the electric mopeds available for hire in the city. The only requirement was to complete a brief theory test on the app.

We'd only ridden a moped together once before. Four years on, Sarah was still traumatised by the experience. This time, she insisted, she would drive. I could have preserved my masculinity and hired my own bike, but it's worth less than the $16 fare. So I hopped on behind Sarah.

It only costs $1 extra to have your partner ride alongside you, but it may cost you your marriage. Travelling 27mph through the dark through unfamiliar city streets was always going to be scary. Doing so as the passenger of someone who has never previously been in control of a moped only made it worse.

Traffic light junctions on steep hills were particularly fraught. From a standing start, the moped struggled to get going again under our combined weight. Sometimes, it didn't even try. On a couple of occasions the wait for the lights to change was so long that the electric engine turned itself off without warning. As a result, when Sarah released the brakes and turned the throttle, we began rolling backwards. I don't know who was more scared - us or the Porsche driver behind us.

When we arrived back at the flat, I released my grip on either side of the seat. My fingers had been clenched so tightly my tendons had seized up and I couldn't open the front door. Somehow, on a day I'd watched England play in a semi-final that had gone to extra-time, it still hadn't been the most stressful part of my day.

22

IT NEVER RAINS…

The final five weeks of Sarah's course was spent on an externship at a medical technology incubator. There were many parts of Sarah's job I struggled to understand, but the most fundamental was the difference between an externship and an internship. It remains a mystery.

When Steve and Lucy returned to the US, one of the incubator's co-founders kindly offered to let us stay in their house with their au pair while they were away. All she asked in return was that we looked after the family pets. Of these, the apple of my eye was Poppy, a strong but gentle black doberman. Sarah meanwhile developed a soft spot for the lab-created bald guinea pig the family had taken in when no one else wanted him. His digestive activity could clearly be seen through his soft, wrinkly, paper-thin skin every time he ate, while the skin's tricolore appearance inspired his name, Neo, due to its resemblance to neapolitan ice cream. Such characteristics would give you top billing in the list of novelty pets in most homes. But this arguably belonged to Leppy. He was a snow leopard lizard roughly the length of a hand span. You can guess which of the pets' names were chosen by the children.

Altogether, it represented quite a step up from caring for the basil plant over the previous three weeks. Sarah's colleague encouraged me to take Poppy out while riding their electric bike. This struck me as a disaster waiting to happen, but Poppy enjoyed the sprints required of her. The surge of power that followed each press of a button felt like an injection of EPO into my bloodstream. Sarah, riding a bog-standard bicycle, was left eating my dust and cursing her luck at marrying such a child. Like many cyclists, I'd long been sceptical of e-bikes, but the fact I would gain little exercise riding them perhaps says more about my own lack of discipline.

The house in Tiburon had access to a neighbourhood pool and a private beach. Late one afternoon we borrowed two paddle boards and walked to the shore. I had found the sport a bit too sedate for my liking the previous time I'd tried it, but on this occasion, it was anything but.

Although the weather was sunny, the persistent strong breeze made it too cold to just wear swimming gear. Sarah took to the water first, wearing one of my jumpers on her first foray on a paddle board. By the time I was ready a minute later, she was already quite far out. I was impressed she'd taken to the sport so effortlessly and rushed to catch up with her.

"Stop! You're going too fast!" Sarah said as I passed her.

I snorted at the absurdity of the observation. It was impossible to go too fast on a paddle board. "Why?"

"We're getting blown further and further out. Your stupid jumper is acting like a sail and I–"

Her words were lost in the wind.

"You'll be fine," I shouted back, though I doubt she heard me.

It's almost always me who is the first to blink in the face of danger. Sarah's conviction that things will always pan out ok, even in the face of mounting evidence to the contrary, meant that if Sarah was worried, I should have been too. But I convinced myself Sarah's distress was down to the fact it was her first time paddle boarding. It struck me as an unusual frailty, and one I'd enjoy teasing her about later.

I began to change direction to head back towards Sarah and the shore. It was only then, a quarter of a mile from the beach, that I realised the truth of her observation. I could turn the board around, yet try as I might, I couldn't get it to return towards land. I was pushing the water back with the paddle as hard as I could, but the wind was too strong. It was taking all of my energy just to stay in the same place. As everyone knows, exhausting yourself in this way is how you die out at sea.

So I stopped paddling and lost precious ground as I considered my next move. The outline of the cars travelling across the 5.5-mile-long Richmond-San Rafael Bridge were becoming clearer and Red Rock Island, a small uninhabited land mass two-thirds of the way across the channel, was getting larger. Sarah was shouting in my direction, but I had no chance of hearing her.

In the time I'd stopped paddling, the wind had turned the board onto its side, accelerating the speed with which I was being dragged off-shore. Trying to correct its orientation, I fell in the water. The cold shocked me. When I was back on the board I stayed on my knees and paddled hard as I shivered in the chill wind. My reduced surface area helped me to finally move incrementally towards the shore. I made it back to the sheltered water by the headland half an hour later, ready to collapse on the sand.

Sarah stood there, looking unimpressed. "I thought you said paddle boarding was boring?"

The week we spent in Tiburon was the final week of Sarah's externship. After saying goodbye to the animals, we set off for Lake Tahoe to begin our summer holiday. The trip had been months in the planning and our excitement had only intensified when another of the incubator's co-founders offered to let us stay in their holiday house in Tahoe.

Unfortunately, everything else quickly unravelled.

While sunbathing on the beach at Lake Tahoe, I noticed a murky greyness growing in the sky behind us. As the day progressed, the sky over the lake remained clear but it became increasingly difficult to ignore the evidence that a major wildfire was under way nearby.

As we walked back at the end of the day, I decided to take a small shortcut away from the road. As I left the asphalt, I stepped onto a piece of discarded construction rubble. It gave way and I turned heavily on my right ankle.

"Aaah!"

"What? Are you ok?" Sarah asked, turning around to face me from a little distance up ahead.

"My ankle. I...I don't know," I said, hopping towards a place I could sit down before I fell down. "It's not good, but...but I'm sure I'll be fine," I lied. Waves of nausea were breaking over me as I took off my sandal and watched my ankle swelling grotesquely before my eyes.

"Oh my gosh," Sarah said upon reaching me and realising the gravity of the situation. "What happened? Have you been bitten?"

I was breathing heavily, trying not to think about how exactly we were going to embark on a walking holiday in the next few days with an ankle the size of a cantaloupe melon.

"I went over on my ankle. I think I heard a crack."

"A crack? We need to get you to hospital."

"No," I said, keen to avoid an expensive trip to A&E. "It's painful, but I don't think anything's broken. I've always had weak ankles. It's just they've never looked like this before."

"Ouch." A young girl with dirty blonde hair had appeared on the roadside above us. She turned to Sarah. "Will he be ok?"

"He'll be fine," Sarah said, trying to convince herself as much as the girl. "Do you live near here?"

"Yes, we live there," she said, pointing across the road. "And our neighbour died in that house."

"Oh dear, that's sad," Sarah said, keeping admirably calm. "Do you think you could ask someone if they have a bag of ice we could use please?"

"Sure, I'll go check."

She came back a few minutes later with a sandwich bag of ice cubes and her intrigued four-year-old brother. I gasped as I pressed the bag to my skin.

"Right, I'm going to go home, get the car and pick you up," Sarah said. "On the way back we'll go to the pharmacy to see if they have anything that will help. Don't go anywhere."

"That would be tricky."

"And don't die while I'm away."

I knew it was at least a half an hour walk back to the house so I settled myself as comfortably as I could. Fortuitously, I'd recently downloaded the free St John's Ambulance app onto my phone, which provides instructions as to what to do in various emergencies. I recommend you do too.

The children watched me from a distance, curious to learn more about this strange-sounding man with one ankle much larger than the other.

"I nearly broke a bone in my big toe once," the girl announced.

"How was it?" I asked.

"Sore."

I clung to the hope that one day I'd refer to this incident as the time I *nearly* broke a bone in my ankle.

When Sarah returned, we drove to the pharmacy, where Sarah bought an ankle support, pain killers and an elastic bandage. These were not the preparations we had been intending to make two days before beginning a 32-mile, four-day hike.

Things got even worse when we arrived back at the holiday house. Sarah had received a text message from her colleague informing her that the au pair we'd lived with in Tiburon had tested positive for Covid. In my condition, the need to isolate wasn't going to be a problem, but the implications for our hike remained unclear.

"I think it's technically ok to go wilderness hiking while isolating," I asserted.

"You're not seriously considering still doing the hike?"

"Absolutely. As long as my ankle's not broken, we should."

"But you can't walk."

"No, but I don't need to right now. Just in two days' time. I can heal a lot between now and then."

"It'll still be swollen."

"We'll strap it up and be careful, but ultimately it doesn't matter what it looks like. It's how it feels."

"You might say it's fine when we leave the house, but what if you hurt it halfway along the route? I can't carry you."

"No, and that's why we'd have to be careful and go a little more slowly than normal. But we've got four days to do 32 miles. We should be able to do it."

"Ok, let's assume by some miracle you recover. I don't think we can go wilderness hiking on the final couple of days of isolation."

"Why not? We're not going to see anyone. The whole point of wilderness camping is that we won't see anyone else."

"I'm not going to argue about this until we need to make a decision," Sarah said, refilling my empty water glass. "If you're somehow walking around here in 48 hours, we'll reassess."

The challenge had been set. This was going to be the most intensive rehabilitation programme since David Beckham broke his metatarsal in the run-up to the 2002 World Cup.

Even if I hadn't been nursing an injury and we hadn't been trapped in isolation, our options would have been limited over the next two days. Smoke from the Tamarack wildfire quickly spread, polluting the air and making it harmful to be outside. Opening the back door for just a few seconds made it feel like we'd put our faces into a blast furnace. So we stayed inside, watching ash fall onto the balcony.

Knowing that the fire could have been suppressed before it spread out of control only increased our frustration. A result of a lightning strike in a rugged, rocky area, authorities had allowed the fire to burn naturally for 12 days. Regrettably, our arrival in Tahoe coincided with the fire penetrating nearby natural barriers and from that point the fire grew rapidly.

Wildfires are more commonly caused by humans, often by halfwits lighting fires at times and locations they shouldn't. At the time of writing, a couple face 20-year prison sentences, charged with involuntary manslaughter and recklessly starting a fire, after setting off a coloured smoke bomb as part of a gender reveal party in California three days before we arrived in the States.

With one foot elevated by cushions and nothing else to do, I searched forums for whether the Tamarack wildfire would make our hike in Desolation Wilderness untenable. The region was less than 40 miles north-west of the fire. A few optimistic hikers suggested it might be feasible as long as we wore masks at all times to protect our lungs from the smoky air. Which wasn't quite how we'd pictured spending our summer holiday. If we were unlucky and the wind changed direction, we would not only be exposed to extremely unhealthy air, but potentially have placed ourselves in the path of the flames. My ankle could now tentatively bear weight, but I reluctantly accepted that, if push came to shove, it wasn't going to be capable of getting us somewhere safe fast. We decided not to go.

Judging by the appearance of my foot in the days that followed, it was probably for the best. The swelling slowly receded, but the bruise extended across my foot like a purple mist, slowly turning green and spreading up my shin towards my knee and down all the way to my toenails. Sadly, while the bruising remained for weeks, the fire continued burning for even longer. By the time it was extinguished three months later, more than 68,000 acres had been destroyed.

Still, we were deeply disappointed we couldn't explore the area's lakes and mountains. A month later, the Caldor Fire devastated large areas of Desolation Wilderness and decimated nearly 800 properties. Prior to 2021, no wildfire had ever burned from one side of the Sierra Nevada to the other, but the Caldor Fire became the second to do so in the space of a month.

Officials implemented mandatory evacuation orders and the roads became gridlocked as 55,000 people fled to safety. The burned wilderness was left more desolate than ever, but it almost certainly saved South Lake Tahoe from far greater damage. The area's granite peaks deprived the fire of fuel and its alpine lakes served as both fire breaks and crucial access points for helicopters to collect water.

Lake Tahoe has long revelled in its picture-perfect all-season holiday destination credentials, where visitors can hike and swim in the summer and ski in the winter. Yet climate change puts this in serious jeopardy. Tahoe's beautiful scenery is at increasing risk from wildfires, and scientists predict the area's world-famous ski resorts may become a thing of the past in the coming decades due to a lack of snow.

After five days in isolation we tested negative. Finally able to resume our vacation, we visited Lake Tahoe's most scenic landmark. The road overlooking Emerald Bay was heaving with tourists desperate to salvage some happy holiday memories after days in which they too had been trapped indoors. Far below, the wake of small boats created faded streaks across the lake's Egyptian blue surface.

The wind was blowing the smoke away from us, towards Nevada, and walking in the sunshine by the water it was easy to forget that firemen were fighting the flames just a few miles away. Only later in the afternoon did a persistent grey haze begin approaching from the east, an unwelcome reminder of how precariously our plans still hung in the balance.

When we had reluctantly aborted our plans to spend four days in Desolation Wilderness, we'd booked a campsite in Tahoe Donner. The destination's name is a reference to the ill-fated westward migration of the Donner Party. They set out from Missouri with hopes of making their fortune in California, but the families' convoy of wagons became trapped by the steep slopes of the Sierra Nevada during the winter of 1846/47. As starvation set in, the group ate their makeshift oxhide snowshoes, while some individuals resorted to cannibalism in order to survive. By the time a rescue team arrived four months later, nearly half of the 87 people who had set out on the journey had died.

We hoped that by driving more than an hour north-west

we would be less vulnerable to changes in direction of the fickle wind. At first we couldn't believe the campground had space for us on a weekend at such short notice, but in hindsight this was almost certainly because someone else had cancelled after watching the news coverage.

The campsite couldn't have been more different from the wilderness camping we had planned. Here, there was volleyball, table tennis and WiFi. There was even, rather conveniently, an industrial-sized ice machine to aid my ankle's recovery. Once we'd set up the tent, we cooked our first boil in a bag camp food. Such products have come a long way since I last used them more than 15 years ago. Butternut dahl certainly wasn't available back then. Unfortunately, in our excitement we failed to account for the 7,000ft elevation. The boiling point of water is much lower at high altitude as there is less atmospheric pressure. For this reason, food needs to be cooked for longer. After eating crunchy chickpeas, it's not a mistake you make twice.

We were careful as always not to leave any food in the car, but the following morning we awoke to find a large paw print on the window and several extensive mud smears. The paw appeared too large to belong to a raccoon, but having watched the videos of bears plundering cars in Yosemite, I was sceptical the Pontiac would have come off so lightly if one had given it a nocturnal inspection.

We headed into the hills of Tahoe National Forest. Atop of a summit at lunch, we watched helicopters fly back and forth carrying water to douse the flames of out of sight fires. The buckets tethered to the helicopters can hold more than 300 gallons at a time, but their minuscule appearance in the vast sky only highlighted their limitations in the battle to extinguish fires that burn thousands of acres of forest per day.

The next morning we walked south past a succession of

lakes. The only movement was the unorthodox mating behaviour of the turquoise damselflies at the water's edge. Initially, we were taken in by the beauty of the intricate insects, but even our untrained eyes quickly realised the heart-shaped 'wheel' the pairs formed while flying in tandem was the closest it came to romance. The males subdued the females from behind by clasping their necks and refused to relinquish their hold even when the females tried to shake them off by dunking them underwater. If this wasn't bad enough, I later learned that females are often bitten during the exchange too.

We'd hardly seen anyone all morning, so it was a surprise when halfway along our route we stumbled upon a large-scale event called Axialfest. Sensing our confusion, one of the organisers explained it was a customer appreciation event for all owners of Axial-based cars. When this explanation was met by blank looks too, he told us that Axial made fully customisable remote control cars. Beforehand, I'd have assumed that a niche event such as this, held in the middle of nowhere, would only attract a small turnout. How wrong I was.

People had travelled from far and wide. We met one couple from Portland who had driven 10 hours to get there. They didn't think it at all strange to get out of their vehicle after such a long journey and immediately want to start driving a tiny car. As we walked around the event, hundreds of people passed us, driving their miniature 4x4s wherever they went. These remote control cars were like daemons in Philip Pullman's *His Dark Materials*, and their conspicuous absence at our feet defined us as outsiders.

We weren't alone though, for the restaurant was a popular stopping point for thru-hikers on the Pacific Crest Trail. The route is more than 2,500 miles in length and runs parallel to the Pacific Coast, from the border with Canada to the US-Mexico frontier. The unseasonably early start to the wildfire season, and speculation regarding its potential impact, was the only topic of conversation among the hikers. In contrast to their dusty, bronzed appearance, the Axialfest attendees were paler, chubbier and decorated in considerably more tattoos.

The organisers proudly told us the event featured 26 courses, each featuring 50 checkpoints for drivers to pass through.

"There's races of all distances to get involved in once you've got a car. The 5k off-road races are particularly popular."

"Do the competitors run alongside their vehicle?" I asked.

"Oh yeah. Some of the times recorded are incredible."

"How long are we talking?"

"Oof, now you're asking. I can't remember, sorry buddy." He extended a bloated arm towards the open can of Coca Cola on the table. I couldn't help but wonder if the times achieved were genuinely incredible - for it's no mean feat to drive a car, however small, while running - or did the times just seem incredible to someone who, in all likelihood, hadn't run five kilometres in the past five years.

"And how much do the cars cost?"

"That I can help you with," he smiled. "Anything up to $10,000 for a limited edition model."

That really was incredible.

Although remote control cars are primarily associated with children, the price showed they weren't the company's target audience. We overheard one man at a stall tell a visitor he considered the cars "an art, a hobby and a business", while another man began a conversation by asking, "You were on my podcast, weren't you?". The community ethos was best summarised by a sticker on the rear window of a parked truck, which proclaimed "Axialfest or bust".

The fierce afternoon heat reflected off the exposed granite as we made our way back towards the lakes. In the distance, the skyline was dominated by an enormous white cloud resembling the head of a giant broccoli. It sounds comical, but this wasn't your average fluffy cloud. It was a pyrocumulonimbus cloud that stretched high into the atmosphere, fuelled by the intense heat of the wildfires below it.

Sarah and I both noticed it, but neither of us discussed its potential repercussions.

23

AN UNPLANNED ADVENTURE

"Do you smell smoke?"

Lying in my sleeping bag, I inhaled, hoping for the best.

"No." Short of a fire inside the tent, this was always going to be my answer. If I refused to acknowledge the possibility of smoke, maybe it would disappear.

"My throat's sore," Sarah said.

"Mmm," I mumbled as I buried deeper into my sleeping bag.

"Can you open the door and see what it's like?"

Ignorance, it seemed, was not an option. I unzipped the tent and stuck my head out. The unnatural orange sun of doom was fighting a losing battle to penetrate the thick blanket of smog.

"So?"

"It's not good," I admitted. "We probably shouldn't hang about this morning."

Sarah was already on her phone, looking up the Air Quality Index (AQI). "It's over 200. Who knows how long it's been like this overnight? We need to leave. Now."

Fortunately, we were already planning to leave Tahoe

Donner for Graeagle that day, where we'd resume our original itinerary.

"Ok," I conceded. "Graeagle it is then."

"Err, no it's not. It's even worse there."

"Shit. Maybe let's risk it today and hope it gets better tomorrow. At least that buys us some time to plan."

"It's currently surrounded by fires," Sarah said, sitting up in her sleeping bag. "It's not getting better and in a tent we're just sitting ducks."

"Fine, ok. Let's skip it. What's it like where we're staying after that?"

"In Johnsville? The air quality is 560. We're not going there."

"This is ridiculous. Is there anywhere on the map we can go?"

"Pretty much the whole of northern California is covered in smoke. Even if the wind changes it's unlikely to get much better and if we stay we'll constantly be checking the AQI. I think we need to go to the Pacific."

We were on our way within 20 minutes. I expected other campers to be making similar moves in the circumstances, but they were either unaware of the long-term health implications, or wilfully choosing to ignore them.

In our rush to reach clean air, we hadn't decided precisely where we were heading. It's rare to set off on a journey without a destination in mind, but with no clean air for 100 miles in all directions, and nearly 400 miles until we reached the coast, we had plenty of time to come up with a plan.

The smoky haze obscured our view of the road and made a mockery of the signposted viewpoints we passed. At one of the few junctions we came across, Sarah waited patiently to allow a car to pull out in front of her.

"That's very generous of you," I remarked.

"Not at all - I'd rather follow him," Sarah said. "He can be the one engulfed by flames instead of us."

The journey required humour as black as the burned trees we drove past. Although we'd escaped the clutches of the Tamarack wildfire, travelling to Donner Lake had brought us within range of the rapidly growing Dixie Fire. By the time it was put out, it had become the largest single wildfire ever recorded in California.

We suspected many of the cars on the road belonged to disappointed families heading home after aborting their holiday plans. As we were between leases on rental properties, we had nowhere to go. Occasionally, while searching for a silver lining, we'd spot a hint of blue sky and celebrate the appearance of faint shadows on the tarmac. The sunshine would vanish within minutes, smothered by the smoke of another fire.

We'd originally planned to visit Mount Shasta. As we drove past we could see fire had ravaged its surrounding foothills, leaving behind only rising smoke and opportunistic vultures eager for a BBQ. It made me recall Sir Winston Churchill's famous quote, "If you're going through hell, keep going".

Despite having lived in California for nearly a year, we'd rarely permitted ourselves the extravagance of air conditioning. But in the baking heat it no longer felt like a luxury. The smoke in Johnsville was 26 times worse than the World Health Organization's exposure recommendation and even in places where it wasn't quite as extreme, it would have been foolish to open the windows or use the external fan to draw air into the car.

Thankfully, after six hours the air quality finally began to improve as we approached the Pacific. En route, I'd read how different the north-west corner of California is to the rest of the state. Yet at first glance it appeared we had simply swapped one grey vista for another, for a cold mist had descended upon the damp coastline. The landscape was as bleak as the opening scene of *Great Expectations*, but at least this shroud of grey wasn't damaging our health.

We pulled into a state park campsite, hoping the rangers might take pity on us when we explained our situation.

"Sorry, we don't have any spaces left," we were told in response. "They were booked up months ago. You need to reserve ahead of time."

"Yes, I realise that," I said, trying to keep my voice level. "Six months ago I reserved spaces in the campgrounds I intended to visit. But we can't stay there now as they might not exist in a few days' time."

"Sir, I understand, but I can't help you. As I say, we've no spaces."

I looked around at the large, unoccupied flat grassy banks either side of the entrance station. "Could we not just stay there?"

"That area's not for camping, Sir."

"Not even just for one night?"

"Sorry, no. Sir, I'm going to have to ask you to move on. People with reservations are arriving behind you."

Sarah turned the car around before I said something I regretted. After a couple more rejections we arrived at Big Lagoon and found the hero we were looking for. The type of person you normally only encounter in fiction, he looked quite the opposite of a knight in shining armour. He had long, scraggly red hair and wild eyes, but these features were softened by the warmth of his toothy grin. He went by the name of Dude and lived among the campers in a small shack by the toilets. Dude apologised for only being able to offer us space above the septic tank, but we assured him we really didn't mind.

Big Lagoon is part of the largest lagoon system in North

America. However, with the thick fog obscuring the views of the water, our first impression was of the striking drop in temperature. Barely an hour's drive south-east, we'd stopped briefly in the town of Willow Creek. There, the heat's inability to penetrate the smog and escape into the atmosphere had contributed to the temperature reaching 37°C. In Big Lagoon, by comparison, it was a brisk 15°C. The contrast was a reassuring, if unexpected, demonstration of how effectively the sea air repelled the encroaching smoke.

We stayed at Big Lagoon for four nights with the intention of resuming our itinerary along the coast afterwards. This section of California's coastline has proved popular with Hollywood directors, but is often overlooked by tourists.

The best known attraction is Fern Canyon, which is only accessible via a bumpy, meandering gravel track through a dark forest. We were the only car in sight and the sense of foreboding was heightened by the ashen slurry that coated the surrounding bushes. It looked like we'd arrived in an overgrown nuclear fallout zone and we nearly gave up altogether when confronted by a river crossing. Attempting to minimise ballast, I got out of the car and watched apprehensively as Sarah drove the Pontiac into the river. As she cautiously advanced, the car's nose pointed ever more sharply down towards the riverbed. Just as I was beginning to question the wisdom of attempting the manoeuvre, Sarah hit the accelerator and the car surged diagonally towards the high ground to the side of the track. The Pontiac's lopsided tilt made it look like a stunt car.

"Never in doubt," Sarah smiled as I hopped back in.

Steven Spielberg described the canyon as an "unforgettable natural wonder" and used it when shooting *Jurassic Park 2: The Lost World*. The eponymous ferns covered every inch of the opposing 50ft high walls, concealing the water running down the rock face. We walked past them through the cool, moist air in awe, while looking up at the fallen mossy trunks that spanned the gorge.

The forest trapped the sea fog and encouraged banana slugs, named in reference to their luminous yellow skin, and northern red legged frogs to emerge. Both were preferable to the two garter snakes we saw.

On the drive back we stopped to admire a field full of elk. Their lack of antlers indicated they were female, so technically they should be referred to as cows. But doing so rather undermines our excitement at seeing them. A better name is *Wapiti*, the term Native Americans used for elk and which translates as 'white rump'. Indeed, in contrast to their sleek brown coats, the elks' bottoms were a spotless light beige, as if they had just sat down on an open tin of paint. I expected such majestic creatures to make a suitably impressive noise, but the sound was a cross between a squeal and the opening of a creaky door. We left with the noise ringing in our ears as we drove a few hundred metres down the road to the town's only petrol station.

Calling it a station is generous. It consisted of a single pump that looked like it belonged in the 1960s. Next to the pump was a necessary explanation on how to operate it, and above it was a sign reading 'Gas: Yes, I really work'. Evidently, I wasn't the first to have my doubts.

The following morning we departed Big Lagoon and headed south to Ferndale. Nestled in a pastoral valley between the redwoods and California's Lost Coast, its location away from Highway 101 has helped to preserve the small town's charm. Ferndale was once one of the state's most productive agricultural regions. Dairy farmers in particular prospered in the 1880s, leading Ferndale to gain the nickname 'Cream City'. The farmers' neighbourly rivalry saw them build a succession of elaborate timber

Victorian houses and many of these colourful 'Butterfat Palaces' remain. Business is a little slower nowadays, as we discovered when we visited the pharmacy 30 minutes after its stated opening time to find the staff inside hadn't got round to unlocking the door.

We continued southwards and along the fabled Avenue of Giants. The towering redwoods bordered right onto the tarmac and the density of the competing trees shut out much of the light. Many tourists just drive through here on the way to their next destination, but that wasn't ever on the cards for us. Even if I was still relying on an ankle support that made it look like I'd escaped house arrest.

In the early 1900s loggers intended to cut down these trees for use as wooden stakes in vineyards, but conservationists argued this was akin to "chopping up a grandfather clock for kindling". Their campaign eventually led to the creation of Humboldt Redwoods State Park, which now contains the planet's largest expanse of ancient redwoods. In total, 137 trees around the world are known to exceed 360ft in height (the size of St Paul's Cathedral in London). All are coastal redwoods and more than 100 of them are found in Humboldt Redwoods State Park. The nearby mountains not only protect the trees from fierce Pacific storms, but also block a large proportion of coastal fog, thus exposing the trees to more sunlight.

The world's tallest tree is not found here however. It grows east of Big Lagoon in Redwoods National Park. Known as Hyperion, it is 380ft tall and, in spite of its stature, was only discovered in 2006. To avoid the tree being damaged by tourists or vandals, its location remains a closely guarded secret.

We admired The Giant in Humboldt Redwoods State Park instead. The tree was proclaimed the 'national champion' at the start of the 1990s, but like almost all champions, it subsequently rested on its laurels and is now 'only' the 19th tallest tree in the world. Standing underneath these colossal organisms, it's often difficult to comprehend their scale and it was only when we walked along a fallen redwood we truly appreciated their size. Approximately a third of the way along the length of the trunk, Sarah spotted a black tailed doe staring back at us. It watched us warily before dancing off into the bushes. The near silence of the forest magnified the snap of broken twigs as the doe's hooves moved across the desiccated fallen leaves. No one else was around and the only background noise was the buzzing of insects, the muted babble of a creek starved of water, and the occasional groaning of the trees as their crowns swayed in the gentle wind.

The fallen trees revealed the root network of these mighty beasts. I'd imagined their roots stretched far underground to anchor them against harsh conditions, but I've battled garden weeds with more depth. The roots fanned out close to the surface, often intertwining with neighbouring trees, as if they were holding hands in support of one another.

Back at the car, we rejoined the Avenue of Giants and arrived at the campground to catch up with our original itinerary. It was nice not to be sleeping by the septic tank, but the campsite was missing a Dude or two.

24

MENDOCINO

A little under 100 miles further down the coast, we reached Mendocino. We walked around the peninsula, enjoying the views of the beautiful coves, arches, stacks and stumps before turning back towards the boutique shops and art galleries of the bijou town centre.

As the waiter finished taking our order at a local restaurant, I asked, "Could we also have two glasses of tap water?"

"Help yourself to water from the cooler on the table," he said. "Please don't take more than you will drink as we are in a drought."

I looked at the thimbles that counted for cups and laughed. Of all the ways water consumption could be reduced, this was surely one of the more minor causes of wastage.

The waiter wasn't smiling though. "It's serious. Take a read of the article by the cups."

Next to the miniature beakers was a photocopy of the front page of the previous week's paper, with the headline 'Mendocino wells running dry'. The story stated:

"The outlook for a town dependent on tourism and hospitality is bleak. Some hotels are already charging extra for daily linen replacement and hot tub use, and other businesses are considering portable toilets to preserve potable water."

After dinner we noticed these policies in action, with one cafe brandishing a sign informing customers that due to the drought they had been forced to close their restroom.

The article in *The Press Democrat* added that local authorities were considering short-term measures such as shipping water in by barge, transporting it by railway or hauling it inside wine tankers. Mendocino County Supervisor Ted Williams admitted:

"From fires to pandemic to drought...I think drought might be the worst."

Of course, the fact that California was experiencing a severe drought was well established. We hadn't seen rain for months. Driving across the state, the falling water levels exposed increasingly large 'bathtub rings' where the rock was usually submerged. Near Sacramento, flooded artefacts originating from the Gold Rush era were revealed as Lake Folsom dried up, while California's second largest reservoir, Lake Oroville, fell to its lowest level since records began.

Yet it was staggering to think this foggy coastal town, that receives visitors from across the planet, had dried up to such an extent. Mendocino is more vulnerable than most as it draws water almost exclusively from a shallow underground water table. The 19th century solution to this dependency was the construction of wooden water towers. Many of these structures remain today, but the rise in the number of tourists over the subsequent decades has only magnified the town's demand for an increasingly scarce resource.

The pandemic had created divisions in the town between the owners of struggling businesses and residents, some of whom were trying to prevent tourists from visiting on the grounds they may be carrying the virus. Now the shortage of water was raising tensions once again. The businesses which had just about kept their head above - ahem - water, were now facing criticism from homeowners rationing their showers. One 82-year-old resident later told *The Guardian* she had been "setting personal hygiene back several centuries".

The situation got worse before it got better. Two months after our visit California governor Gavin Newsome officially declared a drought emergency, with the state experiencing its worst dry spell since the construction of Ferndale's Butterfat Palaces.

Mendocino attracts 2,000 daily visitors in peak season, double the number of residents in the town. Now acutely aware we were part of the problem, we finished our cups of water and departed to our campsite in nearby Van Damme State Park. The park features another, smaller, fern canyon, and as we walked through it the following morning, we passed a series of berry bushes bearing a fruit we didn't recognise. They looked like flattened raspberries and fitted like a pink beanie hat on top of our little fingers. We'd overheard people back at Big Lagoon collecting huckleberries and assumed this was what they were.

At this point I remembered the story of Nicholas Evans. In 2008 the author of the *Horse Whisperer* picked some wild mushrooms with his wife, brother and sister-in-law and cooked the foraged food for dinner. When all four of them began to feel ill the next morning they consulted a book in their kitchen and realised the mushrooms were deadly poisonous. The blame game began and within hours their kidneys failed. They nearly died and all but one of them required a kidney transplant. Their wait to receive them took years and the familial guilt and bitter recriminations lasted far longer.

This was not an experience we wished to replicate. But the fruit looked so ripe and sweet. Surely it wouldn't look so tasty if we weren't supposed to eat it? We gave into temptation and ate a few. They were a strange hybrid; although similar to raspberries in appearance, they tasted like blackberries. It was only the thought of Nicholas Evans and the tragic case of *Into The Wild's* Christopher McCandless which held us back from eating more.

When we regained phone signal, I checked what we'd eaten. It was immediately evident they weren't huckleberries, which, as some readers will know, look more like blueberries. After some panicked research, it transpired we'd eaten thimbleberries. And that we would feel just fine the next morning.

We continued walking along a path through the forest created by the Civilian Conservation Corps. The CCC was the product of a forward-thinking policy designed to provide work and housing for unemployed unmarried men during the Great Depression. The principle of federally funded job creation sounds perilously close to socialism in the land of the free market, yet public sentiment was strongly supportive of the scheme. Between 1933 and 1942 three million men enrolled, and without their contribution many of America's state and national parks would look very different today. For example, much of the infrastructure in

Death Valley exists thanks to the CCC members who performed backbreaking work in searingly hot conditions.

For all of the trails, bridges and buildings the CCC constructed, arguably its most noteworthy contribution was the creation of stone amphitheatres across the country. We stumbled upon one of these while alone in the countryside north of San Francisco. The 4,000-seat capacity theatre looked like a relic from Ancient Greece. We visited another in Colorado. The famous Red Rocks amphitheatre is considered the best small outdoor venue in America and holds nearly 10,000 people.

The path through the fern canyon took us to a pygmy forest. Also known as a dwarf or elfin forest, it resembles a large collection of Bonsai trees. Even though some are more than a century old, the trees are barely 5ft tall and their trunks are only as thick as a finger. This is a consequence of the extremely acidic, low nutrient and poor draining soil, which is estimated to be up to a million years old. Just a stone's throw away, trees of the same species growing in younger, more fertile soil exceed 60ft in height. We enjoyed the novelty of looking down onto the crowns of the stunted pines, but not everyone who comes here does. One reviewer commented:

> "Lots of sick, unhealthy trees. Not so cool. If you hike down to the river it's wayyyyy better. The trees actually grow decently there."

We left Van Damme State Park and arrived in Anderson Valley that evening. After 10 days of camping, we were looking forward to having a roof over our heads in one of California's most celebrated wine regions.

25

ANDERSON VALLEY

As we had on previous wine tasting trips, we planned to walk between a couple of vineyards where we'd reserved tastings. The climate in Anderson Valley is tempered by cool marine air which makes it the perfect place to produce pinot noir. Unfortunately, we'd enjoyed said pinot too much at our first stop and left ourselves short of time to walk the four miles along the main road to get to our second tasting. Seeking an alternative to power walking beside the fast-moving traffic, I suggested we hitchhike.

"We can try. But you've got to ask," Sarah said, suddenly uncharacteristically shy.

I approached two men in their thirties outside a small grocery store. "Excuse me, would you mind giving my wife and I a lift a mile or two up the road please?"

Both men looked apprehensive. "Sorry, we can't. We're only just going round the corner."

"That's not a problem - so are we. Any distance at all would help."

"Yeah, sorry." Both men hurriedly got into their shiny black BMW and sped off at speed in the direction we were heading.

"Maybe we should stick to walking," Sarah said.

"I didn't know I was that scary. Fine, let's just keep going and I'll try to flag down a car on the way."

My attempts to do so were predictably unsuccessful. I was giving up hope when an old Toyota Land Cruiser pulled up at a small junction adjoining the main road. Seizing our opportunity, we asked as sweetly as we could if they would consider giving us a lift.

"Sure, hop in!"

The car belonged to a joyful couple in their sixties named Jim and Helen who seemed as excited to come across us as we were them.

They immediately began peppering us with questions - none of which concerned our destination. In other circumstances, this would have rung alarm bells, but Jim and Helen were evidently just keen to learn all about us.

"I hope we're not taking you out of your way," I said, looking for an opening.

"Don't worry about it. We were heading home, but seeing as you were walking from that direction, we'll get you on your way first."

"Thank you so much. We were hoping to get to Navarro if possible please." This was my mistake. Navarro was the nearest town, a 20-minute drive away. The place we actually wanted to get to was the much closer Navarro Vineyard. Yet Jim didn't bat an eyelid at the prospect of two strangers asking him to drive 40 minutes out of his way. I realised my error just in time. We were dropped off and what had felt like a whirlwind interview was brought to a premature close.

Since getting into the vehicle we had learned almost nothing about our generous chauffeurs. Which was a pity. As we jumped out, they passed us their business card. Our drivers were none other than the Puzzle Purveyors To The

White House. Their products are targeted at toddlers, but I fear solving the puzzles may have been beyond some of the building's incumbents.

We intended to take the scenic route back to our accommodation. This involved walking through Hendy Woods State Park and then along the Navarro River. There didn't appear to be a path on the map that ran adjacent to the water, but at worst I thought we could walk a few miles in the river itself. After all, given the lack of rain, how deep could it be?

Shortly after turning off the main road, we saw a topless man in his early twenties standing on the edge of a bridge. Before we could say anything, he'd jumped.

We heard a splash and ran to the bridge, which was at least 20ft above the water.

"Are you ok?" I shouted down.

"Yeah, bro. I landed with my arms out wide so it broke my fall," he said, looking pleased with his ingenuity. "It's all good!"

He waved to show me the undersides of his arms. Both were already glowing red from the impact.

I respected his bravery, but his reckless decision to jump wasn't going to help me convince Sarah the walk home would only involve paddling through ankle-deep water.

We'd correctly anticipated the unorthodox route wouldn't attract much, if any, footfall. So we were surprised when we came across a wedding photoshoot in the woods. Among the assorted family members were two deeply reluctant young boys dressed in matching suits and a girl of about six in a pink dress.

"Who are you?" she asked as we approached. She had probably half-recognised her various distant relatives when they emerged between the trees, but she'd drawn a blank upon seeing us.

Deep in thought about where we might be able to rejoin the river, and finding it increasingly difficult to disagree with Sarah that this was an escapade my ankle could do without, the simple question caught me off-guard. Who was I?

Luckily, the girl's mum stepped in and saved me from an existential crisis.

"It's ok Becky, we don't know these people."

Becky shot us an unimpressed look, but whether this was a judgement on our scruffy appearance or our lack of blood ties wasn't clear.

We eventually reached the river. Or at least where the river would usually have run. I still have no idea where the water under the earlier bridge had disappeared to, but we were now standing in a 30-metre-wide channel filled with loose rocks, puddles and desiccated mud. It was the kind of place you see when the post-apocalyptic world of the dinosaurs' final days is depicted on TV.

The relief I felt knowing we could complete the journey without wading through chest-high water was tempered by fears the sporadic, shallow pools in the riverbed would be irresistible to thirsty mountain lions. These fears intensified when we pushed back a branch and were confronted by a deer carcass missing its rear legs. Our reaction drew the attention of another deer, who took flight to the other side of the riverbank.

When we eventually returned to the main road an hour later, we were both starving. It was therefore unfortunate that when we sat down at an outdoor table of a local restaurant and ordered giant burritos, they arrived containing a sauce far spicier than I could handle. Upon tasting it on my tongue, my pupils instantly contracted and I began to sweat profusely. By the time I caught the waitress' eye and begged her to bring bucketloads of sour cream, I looked like I was in the midst of an exorcism.

Which, from the perspective of my innards, wasn't far from the truth.

Sarah enjoys spicy food and found my struggles endlessly entertaining. She knows I can't abide food wastage and when she was full, it was left to me to eat what remained. I was soon catatonic and feeling rather unwell. The restaurant had long since locked up, so we hastily walked the final leg of the journey back to the toilet at our accommodation.

Sarah, wisely, asked to go first.

"Ok - but make sure you're quick," I said, dancing from one foot to the other as I waited on the other side of the door.

"Aaah! There's a frog in here!"

"I'm sure he's harmless. Get on with it."

"I can't. He's on the cistern." Minutes went by as Sarah tried in vain to move him.

"I can't wait much longer," I pleaded.

Sarah mumbled something in protest and sat down. Then, while she was washing her hands in the sink, the frog made a fatal miscalculation. He jumped into the toilet bowl.

My efforts to make him move became increasingly desperate. I flushed the toilet in the hope it might provoke a response, but he stoically tolerated the water cascading onto his head. In the end, we both ran out of time.

Trying not to recall the scene from *Snakes on a Plane*, I sat down. The poor frog must not have known what hit him. Which was probably for the best. I flushed the toilet and, this time, he disappeared.

To mark our first wedding anniversary the following day, we returned to the coast for a short walk just south of Point Arena. From the clifftop, we could see dolphin fins cutting through the water and, as our eyes adjusted to the shimmering light, we spotted whales arching their backs as they prepared to dive. The whales were too far out for us to be certain, but their presence in summer strongly suggested they were migrating humpbacks.

To mark the special occasion, we splashed out on a hotel room with a sea view. I'd worried the mist that had dogged us at Big Lagoon would return, but we were able to enjoy the evening sun as we ate pizza on the pebble shoreline. At the front of the adjacent pier, a monument was dedicated to the 15 men from Yawatahama in Japan who landed here in 1913 after sailing nearly 7,000 miles on a 15-metre-long wooden boat. The plaque stated:

Their dreams and courage continue to be a source of
inspiration and a foundation of the friendship
between the people of Yawatahama and Point Arena.

The Pomo Indian Tribe in Point Arena fed the malnourished sailors, but this "foundation of friendship" was sorely lacking when US immigration officials apprehended the men. According to one of the crew, they were taken to San Francisco, where they were soon sent packing back to Japan alongside "100 whores, pimps, drug peddlers and stowaways".

The next morning we too travelled down the coast to San Francisco. I kept scanning the horizon for whales and sea otters, but saw only kelp and variations in the ocean's currents running across the surface like stretch marks.

We stopped briefly for lunch at Jenner, a tiny village of approximately 100 people that overlooks the estuary where the Russian River meets the Pacific Ocean. Within months of our visit, a travel website had declared Jenner to be one of America's top 25 coolest towns. Which I guess makes us trendsetters.

26

A WHOLE NEW BALL GAME

Originally, our summer holiday had been planned as a long goodbye to California. But at the end of her course Sarah had received an offer to stay in the country and work for the PDC. Sadly, this is a different organisation to the Professional Darts Corporation, so I'm still waiting for the opportunity to dress up as a chicken at Ally Pally. In this case, PDC stood for the Pediatric Device Consortium. Sarah's new role would see her focus on designing medical devices to help improve care for children with heart conditions. It was an excellent opportunity to undertake important work, but inevitably lended itself to fewer puerile jokes than a year studying urology.

Needing to find new accommodation in Palo Alto, we temporarily moved into our smallest place yet: a 6mx3m annexe made predominantly of straw. We quickly ran out of work surfaces and prepared all our food on the bare concrete floor. As with all the properties we stayed in, the power supply was limited too. Halfway through cooking dinner one evening, the electricity fused, leaving us with only one working socket above the bathroom sink. After trying and failing to find the fuse box, we called our Airbnb host. She didn't pick up. Feeling hungry and unsure what else to do, we moved the microwave to the bathroom.

10 minutes later, our host called back. "Hey, what's up?"

"Hi. We're really sorry, but we think we've fused the house. We don't have any power."

"Ok, you'll need to go into the main house to switch it back on. There's a key under the–"

BEEP BEEP BEEP rang the microwave triumphantly.

"What's that noise?"

"Err–"

"Is it the fire alarm? 'Cause if there's a fire, the straw will–"

"No, no, it's not," Sarah interjected.

"Right...ok," she said sceptically.

I could hear the silence on the call from across the room as Sarah weighed up whether it was better to pretend the fuse was fine after all, confess to being pyromaniacs, or come clean and admit the microwave was balancing precariously on the bathroom sink. She decided to leave it to the owner's imagination.

Eager to escape the close confines of our hut, at the weekend we cycled from Palo Alto to San Jose. En route, we travelled through Googleplex and alongside the imposing, partially built dark glass premises that represent the latest addition to Google's ever-expanding global headquarters. Less than three miles away, stood Yahoo's own HQ. Duck-DuckGo may have been based there too, but its privacy settings left us guessing. What we couldn't miss was the enormous steel hangar in the middle of the nearby NASA research centre.

The hangar is one of the largest freestanding structures in the world, covering eight acres of land and standing just shy of 200ft tall. It was built in 1933 to house the USS Macon which, along with its sister ship the USS Akron, remains the largest helium airship ever built. These naval scouting airships accommodated 80 crew and were capable of both launching and picking up planes mid-flight. The massive lighter-than-air vehicles were lauded as the future of air travel, but their time in the sun was short-lived. When both airships were involved in fatal crashes within the space of less than two years, the era of the dirigibles was over. The site was vacant for many years, but its appearance remained much the same until 2011, when the structure's exterior panels were removed after they were found to be leaking hazardous chemicals. The process was described by the US Navy as the "biggest scaffolding job in the history of the West Coast". Only the bare skeleton of the hangar was left behind.

NASA subsequently leased the hangar to Google on the condition it faithfully restored the structure. How the company intends to use it remains subject to speculation. In a neighbourhood already featuring several headquarters that resemble the lairs of James Bond-esque villains, this 1930s icon will be as diverting as any.

We continued along the dusty path around man-made salt ponds as we skirted the southern shore of San Francisco Bay. The area attracts few visitors, thanks to the combination of its largely featureless landscape and the noxious smell of decomposing algae in the water. Cycling underneath the long line of pylons, we could hear the unsettling sound of static electricity crackling. While the wetland holds little appeal to Californians spoilt with stunning scenery, it's a haven for birds such as ruddy ducks, egrets and pelicans. Black double-crested cormorants overlook them all, sitting in nests built high in the pylons.

Located 50 miles south of San Francisco, we'd expected San Jose to be full of the hustle and bustle of normal life, filled with people managing without the riches provided by their latest business acquisition.

California has plenty of such places, but San Jose is not one of them.

The city reportedly has the third highest GDP per capita in the world and at the time of our visit, the city's metropolitan area contained the highest percentage of homes valued at $1m or more in the United States. We stopped for lunch at San Pedro Square Market, unable to resist the middle-class bait of a wood-fired pizza oven, craft beers and a live band. The outdoor seating was filled with customers enjoying the sun, but elsewhere the city was almost completely empty. San Jose is the 10th most populous city in the country, yet we saw more people living underneath highway bridges as we approached the city than we saw in the centre itself.

Where was everyone? We'd come to watch Major League Soccer team San Jose Earthquakes play, but, given the MLS is not renowned for its large attendances, it seemed unlikely the game was the cause of the mass disappearing act.

The Earthquakes' ground is sponsored by another of Silicon Valley's success stories, and I was pleased to see the crowds swelling as we approached PayPal Park. I'd anticipated the matchday experience would differ considerably from watching football games in the UK, but it quickly became clear the MLS really was in a league of its own. This was less a football match than a summer fete with a concurrent game of football. The 'fans' seemed far more interested in playing cornhole, drinking mango wheat ale and partaking in wine tasting. In the UK drinking in sight of the pitch has been banned since 1985, so watching football while contemplating the merits of the locally produced cab sav was something of a novelty.

The visiting team were Los Angeles FC, the inner-city rivals of LA Galaxy, who famously signed David Beckham in 2007. Whereas some of the chants from the home team left much to be desired - "San Jose, Olay Olay Olay" was at least easy to pick up - the away fans, dressed in their YouTube-sponsored replica kits, were boisterous throughout.

I'd convinced Sarah it was best to watch the match from the standing section of the ground, where we'd be close to the pitch and where I predicted the atmosphere would be best. However, most of the noise came from Los Angeles' District Nine Ultras, who devoted much of their attention to their club captain and star player, Carlos Vela. The Mexican striker is a former Arsenal protege and I remembered him looking incredibly youthful when he broke into the first team. It was strange to see him 15 years later looking like a distinguished Hollywood movie star. Especially when I realised he's only a month older than me.

There has been a long-running debate regarding the quality of the football played in the MLS. This was probably not a fair game to accurately assess this, as both teams were out of form and languishing in mid-table in the Western Conference. The Earthquakes hadn't won at home for more than three months while LAFC, managed by former US national team manager and Premier League flop Bob Bradley, went into the fixture on a four-match winless run. The extent to which Carlos Vela's talent stood out suggested the level was not high though and I suspected both teams would struggle against Championship opposition in England. Further evidence for this conclusion was provided by the first goal, which went in direct from a free kick taken by San Jose near the corner post. Arriving only 11 minutes into the match, many of the home fans missed it as they were still playing cornhole.

The goal sparked a cacophony of noise. *Rock And Roll All*

Nite by Kiss, the song chosen by the goalscorer, blasted out of the speakers around the stadium. The idea of having songs selected by individual players would be mocked in the UK, but Sarah and I would certainly support the introduction of another form of fan entertainment we witnessed. Midway through the match, the stadium announcer revealed a row in the crowd had been chosen at random to receive ice cream.

"I knew we should have bought more expensive tickets," Sarah sighed.

San Jose's second goal came from a diminutive player named Chofis. He was pacy, skilful and only 5'5, but what endeared me to him most was that he wasn't called Chofis at all. Javier López gained his nickname because of his resemblance to a former teammates' ex-girlfriend named Sofia.

Los Angeles pulled a goal back, but Chofis' strike was enough to give the Earthquakes victory.

27

INTO THE WILDERNESS PART I:
HETCH HETCHY

After failing to find alternative accommodation at anything close to a reasonable price, we returned to the studio we had vacated just a few months before. The only difference was the rent had gone up.

Fortunately, following our stint as pet sitters in Tiburon, our services were called upon again. This time we would be looking after an elderly black labrador called Spanky (yes, really). Spanky's owners lived in neighbouring Los Altos, a town containing not one, but two of the only 11 postcodes in America where the median property price is more expensive than in Palo Alto.

We were introduced to Spanky one Saturday morning in early September. It was so hot we cycled past a gardener who broke off from using a leaf blower in the customary manner and pointed it instead directly into his own face in a desperate attempt to gain some respite. Spanky's owners were keen to show us their swimming pool, but wildfire smoke had caused the air quality to deteriorate. So we stayed inside before heading off to order the cheapest items on the menu in one of Los Altos' swanky restaurants.

When we returned home, we opened the door to find

the entire studio was flooded. The flow of water coming out of the shower drain appeared to be abating, but the floorboards were already under four inches of water. Evidently the foundations weren't level, for most of the water accumulated by the front door, where my new laptop had been purposefully, but disastrously, left on the floor to conceal it from view.

We set about bailing out the water as fast as we could using saucepans and measuring cups. The hazardous air pollution was quickly forgotten as we worked with the front door wide open in the stifling heat. By the time the emergency plumber arrived, I had stripped off to my shorts.

"I dunno if that's a good idea," he said, looking down at our bare feet. "That stuff's come out of the sewer." He put on plastic overalls and stepped into our home as if it were a crime scene.

It didn't take him long to deduce what had happened. A rare storm the night before had caused a large piece of root to block the drain in the street outside, so when our neighbour had taken a shower, there had been nowhere for the water to go. Sitting on the watermarked sofa above the warped floorboard that evening, we were grateful he'd only taken a shower.

We hoped there would be no repeat when we departed a few days later to Hetch Hetchy for Labour Day weekend. We'd heard of the strangely named destination while speaking to a ranger on our previous visit to Yosemite. She told us that for all of Yosemite Valley's charms, her favourite section of the park was Hetch Hetchy. So much so, she named her dog after it.

We were sceptical Hetch Hetchy could live up to such praise. But the prospect of visiting somewhere similar to Yosemite Valley without the accompanying crowds was impossible to resist.

The vast majority of the four million annual visitors to Yosemite stay in the valley, yet the area represents only 1% of the national park. Hetch Hetchy lies 15 miles north-west. John Muir called Hetch Hetchy's resplendent valley a "remarkably exact counterpart" to the one now most commonly visited, but today Hetch Hetchy looks very different to the one he first stepped foot in.

Officials in San Francisco had long recognised the potential benefits of creating a reservoir by constructing a dam at the narrow western end of Hetch Hetchy. Thanks in large part to Muir's efforts to preserve the landscape in Yosemite, Hetch Hetchy was protected by the federal government and it rejected a succession of applications from the city's legislators at the turn of the 20th century.

However, the 1906 earthquake and subsequent fire in San Francisco highlighted the inadequacy of the city's water system and Congress finally relented in 1913. This provoked a seven-year legal battle with environmental campaigners who sought to preserve the glacial meadow and pine trees that lined the banks of the Tuolumne River. Muir described Hetch Hetchy as "one of nature's rarest and most precious temples" and argued that if Congress wished to dam the area, it may as well convert cathedrals into water tanks too, "for no holier temple has ever been consecrated".

Muir's words proved insufficient and Hetch Hetchy Valley was flooded in 1923. Today the reservoir rises nearly 100m above the valley floor, engulfing former waterfalls as it stretches eight miles upstream from the O'Shaughnessy Dam. The reservoir provides 85% of the water supply for the 2.6 million people living in the San Francisco Bay Area and the hydroelectric plants the water passes through generate a fifth of San Francisco's electricity. Without this water, Silicon Valley would become as vulnerable to drought as Mendocino.

Many environmentalists continue to campaign for the reservoir to be emptied in order to restore the valley to its past beauty, but this feels like a pipe dream. Nevertheless, it is unthinkable that such a major industrial project would be allowed to go ahead nowadays. Although John Muir and his fellow activists failed to prevent the destruction of Hetch Hetchy Valley, they succeeded in raising public awareness of the need to protect the country's wilderness. This was a vital step towards establishing the National Park Service.

There aren't any camping facilities in Hetch Hetchy, so the trip represented our first experience of wilderness camping. We'd carefully mapped out our route, but when we reached the entrance gate a park ranger informed us wildfires would preclude us from completing our intended loop walk. He reassured us the fires were under control, but recommended we alter our plans a little. We hastily did so and set off into the mountains with four days of supplies.

We started late in the afternoon, but the heat of the day was slow to dissipate and we were soon running out of water on the punishing 3,000ft climb above the reservoir. The terrain levelled out after seven miles and we finally stopped when we reached the location of a spring on the map. Gasping in the encroaching darkness, we found the pool of water hidden behind a bush. It was no bigger than a foot-bath, but the water was cold and clear.

We put up the tent in the twilight and quickly started boiling the water to cook dinner. When the vegetarian korma was ready, I made the mistake of shining the torch into the pouch of rehydrated food and recalled why my dad calls such dinners sunset food: Ok...as long as you dine in the dark.

Although no one else was around, we knew we weren't alone. There had been several recent reports of bear activity in the area. And these bears came with a reputation. Hetch

Hetchy is the place where troublesome, confrontational bears go when they are relocated from Yosemite Valley. Like a typical city slicker, I was jumping at shadows and kept turning around while wearing my head torch to check we didn't have company. The only thing this achieved was blinding Sarah, but it did at least increase my own chances of making it out alive.

The food for the trip was kept in a 12-litre bear-proof canister which I wedged between two trees far from our tent. Be that as it may, I listened attentively as I lay down in my sleeping bag.

Minutes later, I heard a low growl close by.

I hoped I was imagining it, but when this was followed by a low grumble 30 seconds later, I sat up.

"What was that?" I whispered.

"What?"

"That growling noise. Can you not hear it?"

"No..."

The noise returned again.

"That noise," I persisted.

"Oh." Sarah paused. "That's my stomach."

Relieved, but still able to feel adrenaline coursing through me, I vowed we wouldn't buy dehydrated korma ever again.

Wide awake at 6am, I got up and explored our surroundings. Now it was light I could appreciate the beauty of the meadow where we'd set up camp and listened contentedly to the staccato knocking of wood-peckers as I watched the sun slowly rise between the trees. Every few minutes, the serenity was interrupted by the sound of something falling from the canopy. Each time I tried to identify what it was, all I could see was the cascade of pine needles that followed. So, like an idiot, I went to investigate and was lucky to avoid being struck on the head by a hard, green pine cone. They littered the forest floor and I beat a hasty retreat before the next cone fell.

Early mornings in Hetch Hetchy were the best time of the day. The bright sunlight illuminated the contrasting colours as we walked through glades of tawny, yellow and green ferns. The path briefly crossed a gorse thicket, where we were surprised to see a man walking towards us. Unlike him, Sarah and I were both wearing shorts and doing our best to avoid the thorns.

"I'm jealous of your trousers," I said by way of greeting.

He smiled, before turning to Sarah. "You've got the wrong legs for this."

Sarah smiled back in acknowledgement, but was confused. Initially she assumed it was a critique of a lack of athleticism, yet it seemed a strange rebuke and she decided the comment was intended as a compliment. Either way, he would have had a hard time convincing Sarah to stick to activities that didn't put her legs at risk.

As we climbed, we saw plumes of smoke rising from the trees across the valley. Each outbreak appeared unconnected, indicating they were spot fires, created when the burning embers of a nearby fire were carried by the wind. It took little imagination to appreciate how easily the bone-dry yellow grassland and fallen branches could catch alight.

There were few trees on the ridge itself, providing little respite from the oppressive heat as we climbed to more than 8,000ft. It didn't take long for the weight of the tent and the bear canister on my back to begin to take its toll.

We subsequently learned the daytime temperature remained around 37°C throughout our time in Hetch Hetchy, which explains why I found the going so tough. Sarah didn't struggle anywhere near as much. Her own bag wasn't much lighter than my own and she needed to use less of our precious water reserves to sustain herself. I can only assume she's part camel.

It's hardly a secret that women have a higher tolerance for pain than men. Nonetheless, I gained solace from the results of a pain study Sarah participated in at Stanford a few months later. During the experiment, she was asked to indicate when the pain became unbearable. It appears her pain threshold is off the charts, for the brawny researcher ultimately admitted defeat, having worn himself out trying, but failing, to inflict anything worse than severe discomfort.

"Were you not in agony?" I asked later.

"Well, it wasn't very nice," she said. "But he told me to imagine the worst possible pain and frankly, him putting all of his weight onto my shoulder muscle can't possibly be as bad as childbirth must be. They think I'm a good case study though, so I'm going to participate in another study next week."

Some husbands would have objected to the idea of people hurting their wife in the name of science in exchange for $50 Amazon vouchers, but I knew Sarah's mind was made up.

The limited provision of water determined where we pitched our tent in Hetch Hetchy. At the end of our first full day, I went for a swim in the pond by our tent and then, as we hadn't seen anyone for many miles, enjoyed the novelty of drip-drying nude in the sun. I was just putting my clothes back on when two men asked if we wouldn't mind if they pitched their tent next to ours. If they'd arrived a few minutes earlier, they might not have been quite so keen.

The following morning the path skirted several other small bodies of water as we headed towards Wilma Lake.

We stopped for breakfast at one particularly picturesque spot, where the still surface perfectly reflected the surrounding fir trees and granite peaks. Water boatman moved on the surface, the exaggerated shadows of their abdomen and contact points on the water resembling dog paws on the rocks below. At the water's edge, the parched grass gave way to a muddy shoreline imprinted with the actual paw marks of a large, thirsty bear.

Our journey through this wild landscape was brought to a premature halt when we reached the crest of a hill and were no longer able to ignore the acrid smell and thick haze spreading across the sky in our direction. We turned back in an attempt to stay one step ahead of the smoke.

Back on the exposed ridge, we could see more spot fires had appeared on the opposite hillside. As we turned away from our original course to reach Lake Vernon, I spotted a black bear chasing another through the forest. They stopped upon seeing us and began walking towards us, but to my relief ran in the opposite direction when Sarah pointed at them.

We emerged onto a barren rocky plateau. There was little to interest the bears here. The only movements came from lizards scurrying between loose rocks and small birds darting from one isolated tree to another. Grey and black wildfire smoke continued to billow into the air and it was difficult to avoid thinking that this was perhaps a glimpse 50 years into the future, showing how much of Yosemite might look unless we all make changes to the way we live.

Thankfully, the wind direction had reversed, blowing the worst of the smoke away from us. We had finished the last of our water long before we reached the lake, confident we'd be able to fill it up there. But this wasn't as straightforward as we'd hoped. One half of the lake was now out of bounds due to the wildfires and accessing water on the other side necessitated wading through thick marshland.

Eventually, we located a rocky outcrop we could reach by climbing over hundreds of fallen logs. Exhausted and dehydrated, I was happy to take the rucksack off my sweaty back and set up camp. However, a fire was burning on the hillside half a mile to our left and Sarah didn't rate our chances of making a hasty escape if the fire descended into the basin overnight.

Nightfall coincided with an ill-timed change in the wind direction. The smell of smoke now surrounded us, but it was too late to go anywhere else. Darkness accentuated the drama across the valley and I watched transfixed from inside the tent as a cluster of trees intermittently ignited into flames. My commentary didn't help to put Sarah's mind at ease and, worried by the possibility we would be engulfed by flames as we slept, Sarah stayed awake most of the night.

The air smelled fresher at dawn than when we'd gone to bed, but ash particles were scattered across the roof of our tent, suggesting we hadn't done our lungs any favours.

We packed up the tent and set off back towards Hetch Hetchy reservoir, revelling in the dappled sunlight of the forest. Even though the valley has been dammed, this peaceful north-western corner of Yosemite remains a remarkable place.

Four days later, we were contacted by a park ranger requesting information about our route. They were investigating the disappearance of a lone hiker and believe that as we drove out of Hetch Hetchy, we drove past the man coming the other way. The search and rescue mission involved ground, air and boat crews, but sadly his body has never been found.

28

HOT UNDER THE COLLAR AT HARBIN HOT SPRINGS

Summer had flown by and it appeared my ambitions to live out my wave-chasing fantasies were becoming just that. So when Steve and Lucy invited us to join them at a local surf spot one weekend, I wasn't going to pass up the opportunity.

After hiring the gear, we met up on the shore of Half Moon Bay, about a 40-minute drive from Palo Alto. To my disappointment, the weather bore far greater resemblance to the British seaside in autumn than the setting depicted in song by the Mamas and the Papas.

The surf conditions weren't as beginner friendly as we'd hoped either. The waves reared steeply before breaking and had a tendency to unceremoniously dump novices such as ourselves head first towards the seabed. Sarah had only been surfing once before and repeat viewings of waves sending my feet flying over my head failed to provide much reassurance.

I later learned that 11-time world champion Kelly Slater regards Mavericks, an offshore surf spot barely a mile away from where we'd 'surfed', to be one of the most dangerous places he's ever jumped on a board. It also inspired the 2012 movie *Chasing Mavericks*, the filming of which put Gerard Butler in hospital following a surfing accident.

A couple of weeks later, I convinced Sarah to try again in a different location. The wave forecast for Santa Cruz had looked promising. When we arrived though, we saw the waves wouldn't just be difficult to catch, but downright impossible.

The ocean was as placid as a lake.

Reluctant to give up, we followed a local tip-off and hired boards a short drive around the coast at Pleasure Point. We were promised the waves there would match our level.

Our lack of surfing nous was apparent before we'd even entered the water. Sarah found the 9ft longboard cumbersome to carry by herself and in our ill-fitting, freshly hired wetsuits we formed a surfboard train, with Sarah holding the tails of our boards either side of her hips, while I did likewise at the front with the boards' noses. Although effective, it certainly wasn't a technique we'd seen replicated in films.

People walked past us, offering words of encouragement, such as "Teamwork makes the dreamwork!" and other affirmations you might expect to find on walls in the receptions of corporate offices. You'd certainly never hear such positivity from strangers in Britain towards people taking up half of the pavement.

Our surfboard train came to a halt as I peered over the cliff edge. The beach had disappeared under the high tide and the waves weren't as benign as we'd been led to believe. I was considering how exactly I was going to spin this news to avoid alarming Sarah, when a man approached us and pointed out a local landmark.

"Y'know who lived there?"

I confessed I did not.

"Jack O'Neill."

Still dwelling on the sight of the waves breaking close to the rocks, my mind wasn't as sharp as it should have been upon hearing this name and I hesitated for a split second, disappointing the stranger.

"You know, *O'Neill*. The surf manufacturer," he prompted.

"Oh of course, sorry."

"He lived in this house for nearly 60 years."

"Well, it's a great location."

"Yeah, it's not bad. Anyway, good luck out there. You can do it!" he said, smiling at both Sarah and I before turning to walk away.

We hadn't been in the water long when Sarah, surrounded by a swarm of surfers competing for the break, decided to head back in. She would wait for more favourable conditions on another day. Unable to resist the lure of the ocean, I stayed in the water and surfed. Although I'm not sure Jack O'Neill would have called it that.

After an hour and a half I swam a couple of hundred metres around the headland to a quieter break. Tired from my earlier efforts and fighting the current, this short journey across the floating kelp felt like a marathon. By the time I arrived my arms and shoulders were aching and I remained slumped on the board for some time, trying to read the waves while I caught my breath.

When some of my strength had returned, I moved into position to catch a wave. I looked behind my right shoulder to see the wave slowly rising and turned back towards the beach to begin my front crawl. But what I saw stopped me in my tracks.

My passion for sport bears no correlation to my aptitude and nowhere is this discrepancy greater than when surfing.

Yet I'd lost all interest in the approaching swell, which passed unnoticed underneath my board.

For in front of me was a sea otter.

It was only a few metres away, but wasn't at all perturbed to see me. It was lying on its back, its webbed black feet pointing to the sky, as it attempted to crack open the clam it had collected from the seabed. Upon succeeding, its wet whiskers moved animatedly as it tore into the flesh with its sharp teeth, pulling at the meat as if it was toffee.

Days after this encounter, there were reports a gang of river otters had attacked children in Alaska. I would previously have found the notion vaguely comical. But having seen the size of their 4ft-long seafaring cousins up close, I could easily imagine the trauma of such an attack, especially one that left a child with "fang marks" on their thighs.

Curiously, none of the other surfers seemed to be aware of the sea otter. I found it hard to believe that sharing the surf with otters had become such a common occurrence that it was no longer noteworthy. One surfer rode a wave straight over the top of where the otter had been floating moments before. The otter reacted to the surfer's approach by diving underwater and popping back up to the surface again as soon as the wave had passed, as if it was playing a game.

Only a boy with learning disabilities who was out on the water with his father was as enthralled as I was. He looked at me, wide-eyed with excitement, and pointed in the otter's direction. Equally spellbound, the only thing I could muster in response was to mouth the word "wow". We watched the otter in silence for some time. Occasionally it disappeared, returning to the surface clutching a clam and twisting like an Archimedes screw, as if celebrating its achievement. I was now using my board purely as a perch, from which I spotted three other otters nearby. Navigating between them, I returned to the shore, where Sarah was waiting on the clifftop.

~

After two unrewarding surfing experiences, Sarah was keen to stay inland the following weekend. So we drove two hours north of San Francisco to camp at a retreat centred around a natural hot spring.

The weekend began strangely and escalated from there.

En route to the retreat, we stopped at a small vineyard, where we were served by the owner. His slight frame was offset by long, wild grey hair.

"Do you like it here in California?" he asked us.

"Oh, it's beautiful - you certainly don't get days like this in October back home," I replied. The weekend was set to be unseasonably warm, and at noon it was already more than 30°C.

"You English? Do you work for Facebook or something?" he said, unable to hide the cynicism in his voice.

"No, I work at Stanford, designing medical equipment for children," Sarah said.

This seemed to satisfy him as he evidently had little time for Silicon Valley weekenders. At least we had some redeeming qualities.

"The problem with California," he said, opening up, "is all the smoke we get now."

"Yeah, it's such a shame."

"Of course, it never used to be like this. It's not natural. Until 2018, there were never any fires. None. Now there are thousands each season."

"Yes - other people have told us it's much worse now."

"It is. People say it's climate change–"

Sarah and I nodded in acknowledgement.

"–but it's much bigger than that. We're in the midst of a spiritual war that will last decades."

It was our turn to be wrongfooted. "Are we? In what way?"

"They've been controlling the weather for decades and this is the result."

It wasn't clear who *they* were, but our reaction had obviously belied our status as heathens, so he was reluctant to elaborate further. Subsequent research on questionable quasi-religious internet forums provided some intriguing explanations for the rise in the number of wildfires. These included the theory expounded by Republican congresswoman Marjorie Taylor Green, who attributed the fires to space lasers, while other conspiracists believe they are caused by plane contrails which, they allege, contain chemicals that alter the weather and enable widespread mind control.

After mumbling something about telepathy, the vineyard owner changed the topic to sidestep any further questions. "Where are you heading today?"

"We're staying just up the road at Harbin Springs."

"It's a wonderful place there, very spiritual. It was so sad when it burned down because of the wildfire in 2015."

"Was your vineyard affected?"

"Yes, we lost a lot of grapes that year," he said in a resigned manner, seemingly unaware this contradicted his earlier point.

As climate change believers, to Sarah and I it seems inevitable that California's wildfires will worsen over the coming years and it's entirely possible that within a couple of decades, the state's wine industry may cease to exist altogether. In 2020, much of the yield that wasn't burned by the fires had to be destroyed anyway, as the wine produced by the surviving grapes was so infused by smoke that it tasted like an ashtray. The idea of running a business in the face of such uncertainty seems madness. Particularly if you believe your vineyard is located in the no man's land of a spiritual war that will outlast you.

We wished the vineyard owner well and headed off to the springs, knowing that the likely increase in wildfires in the years ahead will only serve to strengthen his convictions.

~

At the entrance of the eight-pool outdoor retreat at Harbin Springs, a sign states that clothing is optional. This may be true, but it was optional only in the sense that it's optional to say no to a small child who asks if they can show you their latest drawing. In our respective swimming trunks and bikini we both felt extremely overdressed.

After five years of monogamy, it was overwhelming to suddenly see so many examples of the human form in close proximity. We stripped off and tried to act nonchalantly as we strolled from one pool to the next. In reality, we were anything but. Our pronounced tan lines marked us out as nudist newbies and our behaviour betrayed our inexperience as we dipped in and out of every pool to check its temperature.

The temperatures ranged from an eyebrow-raising 46°C to a hyperventilating-inducing 12°C. I spent most of the time in the moderately heated swimming pool, which was large enough to do some lengths. I'm unlikely to become a regular nudist, but feeling my bare body glide through the water did feel undeniably liberating. Even if I did feel like an oversized version of the child featured on Nirvana's most famous album cover.

Many visitors were tourists like us, but the majority were

clearly regulars. Old men with long hair and leathery skin like Iggy Pop showcased their zen mastery by performing naked headstands by the pool, while others sought to outdo each other by recounting memories of what the springs were like before the wildfire devastated the site. As I listened to these stories, I reflected how quickly my inhibitions had disappeared. It no longer felt strange or even remotely sexual to lie scarcely a metre away from other naked bodies.

Embarrassingly, I found the ban on mobile phones, and the connection they provided to the outside world, to be more of a challenge than becoming accustomed to the constant poolside nudity. A sign explained that one of the reasons phones were prohibited was because some visitors were sensitive to the electromagnetic frequencies mobile phones produce - even when they're not in use. I was happy to go along with the spiritualism of the site for the most part, but this explanation left me wanting to put these visitors' astounding powers to the test. Guests were also reminded to refrain from sexual activity and, more ambiguously, 'excessive sexual energy'. Generally, this instruction was obeyed, but I was unconvinced some of the intimate antics unfolding in the far corners of the pools after dark could be strictly attributed to yoga.

Arguably Harbin's greatest claim to fame is its position as the birthplace of Watsu, a form of aquatic massage now used across the world. The term is a portmanteau of water and shiatsu, which I was surprised to learn isn't a breed of dog, but a Japanese pseudoscience.

The retreat has three silent pools and after dinner Sarah and I tried Watsu in the largest of these pools. This involves being lightly cradled as you lie face up in warm water. The fact that I had few reservations about lying naked on the water surface shows how swiftly such behaviour had been normalised.

Earlier that evening in one of the small pools, a buxom middle-aged woman lay on her back in the water, her eyes closed and holding her ankles against her bottom. Her ample breasts floated conspicuously above the water line. As she floated inexorably towards us, Sarah and I looked at each other, unsure of the correct etiquette in such a situation. Our backs were already pressed against the pool wall. I considered gently pushing her back in the opposite direction, but such behaviour felt unspiritual and unbecoming. When the woman was only inches away from us, she suddenly came to.

"I didn't realise I was so buoyant," she said, blinking as my face came into focus.

I smiled weakly in response, but I can't have been alone in thinking it mustn't have been a huge surprise.

I was sceptical of the benefits Watsu would bring, but at the very least it was an extremely relaxing way to watch the stars. The only sounds I could hear were indistinguishable underwater noises and it made me think about what it must be like in the womb.

I don't know what Sarah did when she was holding me in the water, but that night in our tent I slept for almost 11 hours. Little did I know I'd married a Watsu master.

29

TUOLUMNE MEADOWS

The next weekend was our first looking after Spanky. Forced to take it easy by an ageing dog with a bad leg, it felt odd not to be spending the weekend discovering somewhere new.

Regardless of his injuries, Spanky tirelessly followed me up and down each length of the pool in the garden to make sure I didn't drown. A gesture I particularly enjoyed, given he didn't move a muscle when Sarah went for a swim.

The son of Spanky's owners, Mike, popped by occasionally. After learning of our recent trips, he urged us to visit Young Lakes in Yosemite's Tuolumne Meadows. Having explored the under-appreciated beauty of Hetch Hetchy, we were eager to find out whether Tuolumne (pronounced Too-wahl-uh-me) Meadows could match it.

Time was running out for us to visit the meadows. To get there we needed to drive along the Tioga Pass, one of the highest roads in California. The route traverses the Sierra Nevada at nearly 10,000ft above sea level and the road is often closed due to snow. The date it shuts varies each year depending on the conditions, but in previous years it has been closed by late October and sometimes doesn't reopen until the following July.

Keenly aware our window of opportunity was about to disappear for another year, we made an impromptu trip one Friday afternoon in mid-October. We drove through glades of evergreen trees and stopped briefly to admire the glacially sculpted grey domes that surround Lake Tenaya.

When we stopped again, the low afternoon sun no longer reached the forest floor and its rays caught only the upper branches of the trees. The first snow of the season had fallen just days before and the snowmelt was a welcome addition to the gently flowing Tuolumne River next to us. The prolonged drought had exposed a number of deep pot holes in the rock. Inside one, we could see a fish swimming and hoped the river swelled before he outgrew his prison walls. Come spring, he'd learn the world was much bigger, and more turbulent, than the one he'd grown accustomed to.

We followed the river out of the forest, onto the wide, yellow grassland of the meadow. The sun had now disappeared behind the mountains, creating a beautiful salmon pink haze across the horizon. The timing was fortuitous, but I'd underestimated how quickly the light would disappear. We walked the final half-mile back to the car in the dark, taking time only to admire the reflection of the moon in the water.

After descending more than 3,000ft through the darkness, we arrived at Lee Vining, the first town east of the Tioga Pass. It had just turned 7.30pm, but the motel receptionist had already locked up for the night.

"Is there anywhere you would recommend for dinner?" Sarah asked as we were handed the key to our room.

The receptionist paused. "I think everywhere will be closed now, sorry."

The restaurant two doors down, Nicely's, had appeared

open, but the receptionist's reluctance to recommend it as an alternative to starving didn't fill us with confidence.

We'd just taken a seat in one of its maroon leather booths, when a group of five men and women in their forties walked through the door. One of the men looked around and promptly declared, "It's cold, damp and dark. I'm not eating here," and ushered everyone in the group back outside.

It's true that it wasn't glamorous. Nevertheless, they were serving food and the beer was only $2. We hadn't seen such low prices since we left the UK.

Tucking into fish and chips and their self-proclaimed 'colossal' sundae, we certainly didn't envy the five people pacing the streets outside, searching in vain for an alternative place to dine in a town with fewer than 100 inhabitants.

Before we drove back along the Tioga Pass to begin our hike the following morning, we stopped at a viewpoint overlooking Lake Mono, which lies a couple of miles east of the town. At one stage Lee Vining had been named Lakeview. But this was also the name of a settlement further south. To avoid confusion, the town was renamed after its founder, the miner Leroy Vining. To have such an enduring legacy is quite an achievement for a man who died after accidentally shooting himself in the groin while sitting in a bar. It was a particularly unfortunate fate considering his brother was called Dick. Still, Lee Vining is a better name than at least one of the alternatives. The area was previously known as Poverty Flat on account of its unfavourable conditions for agriculture.

On the drive back into Yosemite National Park we were able to appreciate the stunning views we'd missed the night before. We didn't even mind that we were stuck behind a motorhome towing a 4x4. At least that's what we think was happening. The driver of the 4x4 might just have been tailgating the motorhome in the hope of slipping into Yosemite without paying the entrance fee.

After leaving the car, we walked through the dew glistening in the long grass until we were above the meadows. There, the low-level scrub at our feet was occasionally replaced by smooth granite, dotted with rounded boulders large enough to hide behind. Above us, the clear blue sky was scored by the contrails of distant aircraft. The vineyard owner would have been worried.

Up until this point the walk had been enjoyable, but not spectacular. I began to privately wonder whether Mike was keen on hiking to the same extent as several other Americans we'd met. Just like almost every man thinks he's handy at table tennis, lots of people think they like hiking. But in reality, their excursions rarely extend beyond a couple of miles.

My scepticism melted away when we saw the cyan water of Lower Young Lakes between the pine trees. The trees formed a crescent around the lake and in the remaining gap, ragged, snowy peaks rose steeply. At the far side was a beach, and it was with great difficulty we pulled ourselves away to visit Middle Young Lake and Upper Young Lake. The two lakes were only half a mile from the first, but it was evident from the lack of tracks in the snow that few people found the motivation to do so. It was worth it though. At Upper Young Lake we looked down upon the other two lakes and across to the Cathedral range, home to some of the highest summits in Yosemite.

On our return to Lower Young Lake to eat lunch, Sarah stated her intention to go swimming. We hadn't even considered the possibility that morning, and I was happy to remain paddling in the staggeringly cold glacial water. But when Sarah went swimming, I once again felt compelled to follow suit. We hadn't seen anyone for hours and the danger of being spotted skinny dipping by anything other than a striped chipmunk seemed remote.

The shock of the water temperature made my skin tingle and Sarah didn't even try to hide her amusement when I got out.

"I've never seen it look so small!"

Neither had I.

After using a spare jumper to dry off, we tucked into the turkey and cranberry focaccia sandwiches we'd picked up from the cafe adjoined to our motel. Enjoying the warmth of the sun, the memory of the turkey sandwiches we'd eaten in The Narrows in Zion on Christmas Day felt a long time ago.

On the way back there was just time for a detour to Dog Lake, where the trees, mottled grey peaks and empty sky were reflected perfectly. Normally, I'd have been eager to skim a few stones, but doing so on such a flawless surface felt sacrilegious.

As we continued our descent, the sun sank behind the mountains opposite us, casting rays of luminous bright light between the silhouetted summits. Beautiful as it was, we heeded the lesson of the day before and walked briskly back to the car.

Usually, there's no reason to pause at the gates when leaving national parks. We did so, but only out of a lingering sense of guilt for having once failed to return a ranger's wave. When we pulled up to see if there was anyone inside the small wooden lodge, a sign in the window read:

The Tioga Pass will close at 4pm tomorrow due to an
incoming storm

When we'd left home on Friday, we hadn't realised we would be cutting it so fine. Still, the deadline wasn't going to stop us from fitting in another hike the next day before we returned to Palo Alto. Our route was just east of Yosemite, in Inyo National Forest. Although less celebrated than Yosemite, the forest contains incredible scenery of its own and stretches over an enormous region, reaching into Nevada and encompassing the area around June Lake. It also boasts the world's oldest individual tree, Methuselah, which is estimated to have germinated in 2832 BC.

Not long after we turned off the main road the following morning, the asphalt disintegrated. We fell into an uncomfortable silence, desperately hoping that the car's suspension wouldn't collapse before we reached the trailhead. Sarah carefully inched the car forward, but our heads still moved like nodding dogs and we winced every time we entered a ditch.

Many of those who drove across the dirt road of the Tioga Pass prior to its modernisation in 1961 had similar experiences. One driver described the journey as "the most exasperating I have ever driven...it is a good deal like a rollercoaster, only rougher!". The American Automobile Association itself admitted "It is not unusual to find people...unused to mountain roads, who just go to pieces, freeze at the wheel and park their cars in the middle of the road to wait for the park rangers."

We knew the nearest ranger would be miles away, so were relieved when we saw asphalt up ahead. However, the pot holes and loose gravel returned around the next bend and we swiftly resumed our private incantations.

Sarah pulled into the car park 25 long minutes later. It was a sunny morning, but a potent wind was already building, dragging the anticipated storm towards us.

This time we'd packed our swimming gear, but as we put on our gloves, Sarah conceded even she wasn't tempted to enter the water. The route took us around Twenty Lakes Basin. We'd hoped to see the snowy mountains and trickling waterfalls mirrored in the lakes' reflections, but such aspirations were blown away by the gale, which whipped up white horses on the water.

We saw more lakes than people that day. One of the few individuals we did encounter was an old man with bushy white hair. He smiled as we approached and said, "Time for one last hike," in reference to the changing seasons. At least, I think that's what he meant. I hope he wasn't ill. He was only wearing a T-shirt, so either way, he wasn't helping his chances of survival. Perhaps he was from Newcastle.

Returning to the car, we joined a queue of drivers at the entrance to the Tioga Pass, all desperate to avoid having to take an alternative route that would add hours onto their journey. The pass closed shortly after we were waved through and didn't reopen for two days. Soon after that, it shut for the season.

30

THE LOST SIERRA

We spent our second Thanksgiving weekend exploring Plumas National Forest in the Lost Sierra. If you've never heard of it, you're not alone. No one we spoke to prior to the trip had heard of the place. It is so 'lost', the destination we travelled to doesn't even feature in the *Lonely Planet* California guidebook. And yet it is one of the most extraordinary places in the Golden State.

Just like Big Sur, the Lost Sierra is tricky to pinpoint on a map. It's roughly an hour and a quarter north-west of Lake Tahoe, which is just far enough to deter the vast majority of tourists from venturing beyond the lake's ever-popular shoreline.

We started driving at dawn and broke up the journey three hours later near Auburn with a 10-mile hike along a fork of the American River. The discovery of gold next to the river in 1848 sparked the gold rush that led California's population to grow from approximately 8,000 in 1840 to more than a quarter of a million people 12 years later.

We saw more families at the start of the walk than we usually would. All were enjoying the crisp morning air as they built up an appetite for Thanksgiving turkey and pumpkin pie. It reminded us of our own families' traditions of going for a walk on Christmas Day.

Shortly before sunset we drove through Graeagle, the village we'd been prevented from visiting by the wildfires in the summer. Either side of the main road, 20 identical red single-storey wooden huts were spaced five metres apart. It looked like we had arrived on the set of a Christmas movie.

Our Airbnb accommodation in Blairsden was only five minutes further on. When we entered the small, cold bungalow, Sarah hastily put on her coat and gloves to unpack. She kept the portable radiator close as she moved from room to room, so that it appeared to follow her like a besotted puppy. I, meanwhile, focused on lighting a fire. It was as if we'd arrived at the dilapidated rural house taken on by the family in *The Railway Children*.

The property owner's instructions were written in riddles, but the statement 'DEER EVERYWHERE' was unambiguous. Sure enough, while eating breakfast on the ramshackle terrace the following morning, we saw five deer in the pasture below us.

In spite of the abundance of wonderful scenery in California, car parks at trailheads fill up quickly. But this wasn't a problem in the Lost Sierra. Even though it was a national holiday in a landscape equal in beauty to Yosemite, we had the place to ourselves.

We walked through Plumas National Forest towards the 7,800ft summit of Mount Elwell. The snowline lay a few hundred feet below the peak. Due to the unseasonably warm daytime temperatures, snow hadn't fallen in the region for a few weeks and we were relieved to find the snow that remained had compacted.

At the top we admired the alpine lakes dotted between the pine trees. The colour of each varied, from an alluring deep blue to white emulsion, depending on whether its surface had frozen. The largest body of water, Long Lake, had an island in the middle and resembled a smaller, wilder version of Emerald Bay at Lake Tahoe. As the tallest of the surrounding peaks, the panoramic view from Elwell was superb, but my eye was drawn to the summit of Mount Lassen, more than 100 miles to the north-west.

As we began our descent, we realised we were running out of time to return to the car before the gate to the main road was locked at sunset. Our attempts to pick up the pace were hindered by the slippery frozen rivulets which spread like a delta across the path.

We were still not out of the woods when the sun set. That the day was over was emphatically emblazoned across the sky. A swathe of intense pink light with the unnatural glow of a highlighter pen backlit the neighbouring trees.

The colour had faded by the time we reached the Pontiac. In the semi-darkness we followed the off-road track back to the gate as fast as we dared. Gratifyingly, we hadn't been locked in. Thankfully, all's well that Elwell.

Eager for more, we returned the following day to explore a few of the lakes we'd seen from afar. In Blairsden that evening, we visited the village Christmas market. Many British people would privately mock their neighbours for decorating their Christmas tree in November, but in the US citizens were already getting into the festive spirit. Much to Sarah's delight, radio stations had begun playing wall-to-wall Christmas songs and countless vehicles passed us with trees strapped to their roofs or hanging out the back of trailers.

Fewer than 40 people live in Blairsden, yet there was no doubting the popularity of the market, the bakery, the craft brewery or the village's pizzeria. Everywhere we went, everyone knew everyone and people knew we weren't residents before we'd even uttered a word.

We were discussing how different it must be to live in such a close-knit community when we turned down the narrow lane to our accommodation. As we did so, we saw a hooded silhouette emerge from the side of the house.

"Are you the Airbnb guests?" a woman asked.

"Yes."

"Just to let you know we're clearing everything from the property..." My mind started to race. Had the house been repossessed?

"...The bungalow and the place next door have just been sold," the woman without a face explained. "Everything has now been cleared from the outside. We'll go through everything inside after you've left."

Relieved, we unlocked the front door. Sarah heated some pre-prepared bolognaise while I lit the fire. Now it made sense why the house felt a little worse for wear. Evidently, our review counted for considerably less than the income we provided.

31

MATCH DAY

It was always captivating to watch a live rendition of *The Star Spangled Banner* in the United States. In sports stadiums, thousands of people would immediately stand in total silence as a young girl sang the lyrics they all knew off by heart. Extreme patriotism lends itself to ridicule, but after witnessing the pride people felt upon hearing America's national anthem, it was hard not to conclude such displays highlighted the need for some British citizens to reassess their feelings for their homeland.

Our opportunities to experience such events had been limited by the pandemic during our first year in California. Now restrictions had eased, I was eager to make up for lost time.

At universities across the US the level of investment in sport is of a different magnitude to that in the UK. For example, the Stanford Cardinals' home ground has a capacity of 50,000 people, yet this is small fry in comparison to other university stadiums across the country. The importance of college football is demonstrated by the fact 10 of the stadiums exceed the 90,000-seat capacity of Wembley Stadium, the largest arena in Britain.

Admittedly, the ground was far from full when we watched the Cardinals host the Utah Utes. One of the reasons for this was that the home fans weren't optimistic about their team's chances as Stanford hadn't beaten Utah for more than a century.

Before the match started, many fans were tailgating outside the stadium. We were initially perplexed when invited to tailgate, as in Britain it's something to avoid doing. In this context though, it refers to the opportunity to have a few drinks in the car park prior to the game.

We anticipated tailgating would be a relatively informal affair, principally involving students leaning against their vehicles. But it was clearly a *thing*. Many people had set up large tents and BBQs to feed their extended families. To some, tailgating was more important than the game itself. Even those who considered themselves supporters were not averse to occasionally skipping matches to carry on drinking. One told me they simply relied on the noise of the crowd and updates on their phone. Such measures weren't going to suffice for Utah's fans. Many of them had travelled 800 miles to be there.

As a sports fanatic, several of my friends expected me to become a passionate NFL convert upon arriving in the States. Yet the sport still leaves me cold. The athleticism of the players is beyond doubt, but the stop-start nature of the games and the frequent changing of the players on the field made the action difficult to follow, never mind love.

Nonetheless, even in a half-filled stadium, it was quite the spectacle. The 60-odd players in the home team squad ran out of the tunnel wearing their traditional red jerseys, white helmets and long white shorts. Either side of them, smoke cannons fired and the university band performed as the players ran towards enormous banners in the middle of the field.

As had been predicted, the first half wasn't pretty for Cardinals fans, with Stanford 38-0 down at the interval. Cheerleaders did their best to entertain the crowd with their extensive, well-rehearsed routines, but it was the band who stole the show. Their modus operandi was summed up by the university's former band director, Dr Arthur Barnes, who stated, "We don't march. We scatter." The band has occasionally been in hot water for taunting their opponents and past controversies have seen them prohibited from playing at some universities. On home turf, they looked to be having a great time as they danced in the stands while performing various pop songs. Considering the long-term health risks posed by playing American football, I would much rather have been in the band than on the pitch. Even if it did carry less kudos at parties.

While checking out the various fast-food caterers in the stadium, we passed several large pictures of Cardinals who had been picked for the honorary All-American football team. As was to be expected, I didn't recognise many of the names. The only exception was Andrew Luck. The quarter-back's prodigious talents had led him to be hailed as the next star of the NFL and excitement about his potential made it across the Atlantic into British publications. In 2012 Luck was duly selected as the number one draft pick. This was given to the Indianapolis Colts as they had the worst record in the NFL the previous season.

Supporters of the Colts and several other struggling franchises had been so desperate for their team to acquire the hotly rated youngster that they actively encouraged their team to lose their last few games of the season. The campaign became known as 'Suck for Luck' and it was the inspiration behind later campaigns such as 'Tank for Tua', 'Bungle for Burrow' and 'Choke for Chase'.

The second half was only a little better for Cardinal fans.

Stanford scored a touchdown but ultimately lost 52-7. The fact that one of the high points was the introduction of a 'drum cam' midway through the game, which showed fans beating imaginary drums in the stands, showed the result had long ceased to be in the balance.

At the start of December we attended a basketball game and completed the triumvirate of America's most popular team sports. The Golden State Warriors were playing at their newly built stadium against San Antonio Spurs. We were supporting the home side, which made us adopted citizens of Dub Nation. The mention of Dub Nation by the stadium announcer drove the fans into a frenzy, but bewildered us. 'Dub', it turns out, is short for 'W', the first letter of the team's 'Warriors' nickname.

Once again, the entertainment surrounding the game surpassed anything found in the UK. Fire machines and personalised videos on the big screen accompanied the name of each of the home team's starting players. The biggest cheer was reserved, unsurprisingly, for the Warriors' star player, Steph Curry. The seven-time NBA All-Star was just 28 three-pointers short of breaking the all-time record.

Despite all the fanfare, the 18,000-seat capacity stadium was once again barely half full at the tip-off. Yet in the time it took for fans to file in from the food stalls, we'd decided basketball was a much better spectator sport for neutrals than either baseball or American football. It's both easier to understand and more exciting to watch.

At times the game felt secondary to everything else going on around it. Fans were asked to vote for the genre of music played over the loudspeakers and cheerleaders ran onto the court to perform whenever a timeout was called.

These timeouts only lasted 75 seconds, but woe betide the possibility that the fans' attention may waver.

The partisan crowd were particularly vocal when the players stepped up for free throws. When the Spurs were throwing, boos echoed around the arena, followed by loud cheers if the thrower missed. Conversely, when Steph Curry stepped up to the foul line, a chant of "MVP" reverberated around the stadium. This is in reference to his record as a two-time winner of the NBA Most Valuable Player award. The pressure on free throw takers is always palpable, and I wasn't convinced the home fans were helping to alleviate the pressure by reminding Curry that he was, in their eyes, the greatest player in the league.

Coming into the game, the Golden State Warriors were top of the league and had an 11-game winning streak. As such, the Spurs were expected to be dispatched with relative ease as Steph Curry inched closer to the historic three-pointer mark.

It didn't work out that way.

Curry's buzzer beater from near the halfway line helped the team claw back a 22-point deficit, but it was the Spurs who claimed victory. The Warriors had the last laugh though. They finished the season as NBA Champions for the fourth time in eight years.

32

COLORADO

Choosing to live in our modest studio enabled us to save enough money to visit Sarah's relatives in Colorado at Christmas.

We'd booked to go skiing but the lack of snowfall put this in serious jeopardy. Snow didn't arrive in Denver, the state capital, until 10 December, shattering an 87-year-old record. With little further snow anticipated until January, Sarah's colleagues joined thousands of others in aborting their travel plans. Lacking any alternative ideas, we stuck to our guns.

After a few days in Denver, we borrowed Sarah's relatives' Mini Cooper Sport to explore the countryside around Boulder. Two days before Christmas, we travelled north towards Estes Park on the edge of the Rocky Mountains. We broke up the journey with a hike around Brainard Lake. The trailhead was at the top of a steep hill and it was with a mixture of joy and apprehension that we saw snow falling as we pulled into the car park. When we had asked Sarah's relatives about the need for snow chains on the tyres, they'd dismissed it out of hand. But now our elevation had doubled, we couldn't help but notice the increased snow on the ground and that every other car on the road was a 4x4.

Still, we figured as long as we didn't stay too long and made sure we returned before dark, we'd be able to make our way back down towards the main road, where we could drive in the tracks of other vehicles.

Snowflakes fell all around us and the only sound was the soft crunch of our footsteps as we walked through narrow corridors of pine trees. The snowfall of recent days concealed sections of ice that had us dancing in our boots, yet this was nothing compared to the hazard posed by hidden streams, as I found out when my foot plunged through the snow into the river.

During our time in Boulder we'd been urged to visit Brainard Lake to see the impressive mountains all around it, but they were almost completely obscured by dense cloud. Snow soon began to fall heavily and we returned to the car in the early afternoon, playing it safe to ensure we got going while there was still plenty of daylight. It was just as well we did.

The car was only a few years old and had numerous features the Pontiac did not. For a start, it had central locking, which I used to unlock the boot. Unbeknownst to us, this was the battery in the key fob's final breath. We couldn't even unlock the passenger doors to get in. Sarah had to crawl over the skis and the bags packed on top of the folded down seats to open the front doors from the inside. Doing so set off a shrill alarm that undoubtedly sent any nearby moose heading for the hills.

Getting into the vehicle wasn't our biggest concern however. Unlike any other car we'd ever driven, the engine was started by holding the key fob next to a button on the dashboard. We frantically searched the car manual to learn how to start the car in the event the fob battery died. The only instruction was to hold the key fob near the steering wheel. That didn't work.

The day before, the fob had given us one warning that the battery level was low, but as we were far from civilisation we decided, not unreasonably, to assume the battery would continue to function for at least a little longer. Its sudden demise left us stranded in the wilderness at more than 10,000ft, in -7°C, with neither phone signal to call anyone for help, nor internet access to find a solution. We were stuck.

Our Christmas angel arrived in the unexpected form of a small woman in her sixties named Wanda. She was returning to her car with a huge Bernese Mountain dog when I approached her seeking help. Appreciating our predicament, she drove us down the mountain until we had enough signal to call Sarah's relatives for advice. They didn't have any suggestions and the Mini helpline could only point us in the direction of the nearest BMW garage in Boulder, a 40-minute drive away. Wanda kindly drove us there, chatting all the way.

"So this is Bugatti," she said pointing to her canine companion behind her. "You can call him Bu."

Wanda had a big car, but Bu still dominated most of the space in the back. Travel fans were hooked up to the handles above the lowered passenger windows, blowing additional cold air directly onto our necks.

"Bu just loves the snow, but he'll overheat if he's in the car too long," Wanda explained. "Holla if you're cold and I'll raise the windows." In our haste to get into Wanda's car, I'd forgotten to bring my jacket, so I was indeed very cold.

"Don't worry, it's fine," I lied. Bu didn't seem too perturbed by the unexpected turn of events, but I would have felt deeply ungrateful mentioning my discomfort considering Wanda was doing us such a big favour.

"You guys jump out and get your battery fixed," she said as we pulled into the BMW garage. "Bu and I'll be waiting here to take you back."

"Thank you, that's very kind. You've already gone above and beyond, so please don't feel you have to," I said.

"Happy to help. There won't be any public transport back up the mountain and no taxis will take you neither. We've come this far, we're seeing it through to the end now."

Equipped with a replacement battery, we headed back up the mountain. As we climbed the nearly 5,000ft in elevation, rain turned first to sleet and then to snow.

"Do ya think you'll get a dog when you head back to England?"

"We'd like to, but cats are definitely easier to look after," Sarah replied.

"True, but dogs can do more for you. With Bu, for example, I take him cross-country skiing with me. When he's pulled me far enough, I'll tell him 'home' and he'll bring me back to the car. Maserati, the Bernese dog I had before Bu, could do the–"

The car's engine gave an indignant groan as the severity of the incline increased. "Oh come on Emilia, not today," Wanda pleaded. She listened out for further protests before resuming. "Where was I? Ah yes, Maserati. He was the same."

"That's amazing," Sarah said.

"It's just a matter of training."

I hoped Emilia would prove to be as reliable.

Every mile was taking Wanda further from her house. All the time, the weather was becoming progressively more extreme. But she showed no sign of resentment. Sarah was sitting in the front seat and Wanda chatted to her animatedly. I kept quiet, fearful about what we would do if, having replaced the key battery, the car still didn't start. The journey to Brainard Lake had been the first time I'd driven the Mini and I began to question whether I'd correctly turned the engine off. If I was at fault for having inadvertently drained the car's battery, all of Wanda's efforts would be for nothing. I was also tormented by the fate of the laptop I'd left in the Mini. We'd been unable to lock the car, so we were relying on the accumulating snow on the windows to conceal the value of the belongings inside.

Assuming we could start the car, I'd remained bullish about its ability to handle the snow on the road. However, when Wanda's 4x4 skidded as she rounded a sharp corner, I began to harbour doubts.

When we finally turned into the car park, we saw our car was the only one there and was buried under more than a foot of snow. The laptop and skis, at least, were safe.

To our immense relief, the car started immediately with the new battery and I set about grabbing armfuls of snow off the windscreen, bonnet and lights. It was a difficult balance trying to fully express our gratitude to Wanda, knowing that with every passing second the journey down the mountain was becoming more treacherous for all of us. Wanda wouldn't even accept petrol money for her trouble and made sure we made it safely back down to the main road by following us all the way with her hazard lights on. Anxious not to damage the borrowed Mini, we drove at a snail's pace, so this was an amazing gesture in and of itself. At the junction, we waved Wanda goodbye and resumed our journey to Estes Park.

Earlier that afternoon, before events overtook us, Sarah had volunteered to drive. The relatively straightforward 45-minute stint she had signed up for turned into a nerve-racking three-hour journey through the dark as she dodged cars being towed out of snow banks by road assistance vehicles. Even the full beam headlights were of little help. They merely illuminated the falling snow, making it look like we were travelling through a meteor shower at the speed of light.

We arrived at an outdoor equipment store just in time to hire some much-needed winter hiking gear and pick up a few trail recommendations. After eating at a restaurant close by, we reached our accommodation and collapsed. It didn't bear thinking about what might have happened if we hadn't met Wanda. Her generosity made us reflect on how we would have reacted if the roles were reversed.

We've tried to find Wanda's details online to articulate our thanks, but so far we've been unable to locate her. If anyone knows a dog trainer named Wanda who lives in Boulder, please let us know. This book is dedicated to her.

The assistant at the outdoor equipment store had advised us to arrive early at Rocky Mountains National Park, but when we nervously asked the ranger at the entrance gate at 8.30am if there would still be parking available, he laughed.

"You won't have a problem," he said, waving us in. "Just watch out for the snowy conditions."

Due to its popularity, the road into the park hardly ever closes. But perhaps it should. At first, we were perplexed by the number of 4x4s driving in the opposite direction to us. We'd assumed everyone was there to go for a walk, but it was clear some people were just out for a drive. To them, it was almost a sport in itself to test out their car in the extreme conditions. The roads hadn't been snow ploughed and, while it wasn't quite bumper cars, it wasn't far off. There was no space to turn around and stranded cars were scattered across the road.

Sarah's experience the previous evening made her the

expert at handling the winter conditions, so my role was simply to plead with her - no matter how terrifying the speed of the car coming the other way appeared - not to stop. If we did, we too would become stuck. The obnoxious behaviour of one driver gave Sarah no choice though, and as the car disappeared in our rear-view mirror, we were left marooned on the ice.

Straining every sinew, I pushed the car forwards until it gained traction. It might have looked impressive had I not immediately slipped in my trainers and fallen flat on my face when the car lurched forward.

My next challenge was getting back in the car.

I opened the door, but couldn't move fast enough to throw myself in. "Slow down!"

Sarah duly did as requested.

"Don't stop!" I said, throwing my left leg into the footwell and dragging the rest of my body in, before shutting the door. "Phew. Go, go, go!"

We kept climbing and pulled into the first car park we saw, hopeful that the road would be cleared by the time we returned down the mountain.

The only problem was that none of the snow from the previous night had been cleared and other than an icy thoroughfare, the car park consisted of a 3ft tall snow bank. In her haste to get out of the way of other vehicles, Sarah drove straight into the pile of fresh snow, embedding the car up to its wheel arches.

Now we really were stuck. Thankfully, we managed to reverse with the help of some bystanders armed with shovels. With nowhere to park though, we had no choice but to drive straight back the way we had come. The sheer stupidity of opening the national park but not providing any space for cars was astonishing.

Just two hours after departing we returned to our

accommodation, feeling drained but relieved to have made it back in one piece.

"Do you have any suggestions of hikes we could do instead that don't involve driving?" Sarah asked our Airbnb host.

"Sure. You can walk through the neighbourhood, up to Deer Mountain. I shouldn't tell you this, but Tommy Caldwell lives nearby, so who knows, you might be walking in his very tracks."

For those unfamiliar with the name, Tommy Caldwell is one of the world's most famous climbers and has appeared in films such as *The Dawn Wall* and *Free Solo*. Although we didn't get to meet Tommy, we had an even greater thrill. Amongst the beautiful wooden mansions, we saw a magnificent bull elk. He lifted his head at our approach, but was content to watch us from a distance as we admired his thick, pointy antlers that were as wide as my arm span. Bears are brilliant and sea otters are super, but standing in the presence of this elk eclipsed them both.

We'd bought microspikes at the shop to help us adjust to the unexpectedly snowy conditions. Their metal teeth and elasticated frame gave them the appearance of something you'd find at an S&M party. Microspikes are designed to be worn underfoot to provide extra traction, but in the virgin, shin-deep snow, they were about as useful as a pair of handcuffs. Evidently, we weren't walking in Tommy Caldwell's tracks. He would be walking in ours.

Around us, the snow had accumulated on clusters of nascent pine cones, giving them the appearance of white baubles on a Christmas tree. Halfway up the mountain, we paused for a duel, each of us wielding metre-long icicles we'd broken off a rock. The icicles shattered upon impact, but our disappointment was tempered by the sight of the clouds lifting across the valley to reveal the peaks of some of the Rockies. The view lasted little longer than our ice swords. A snowstorm hit as we reached the top and the hard-earned views were identical to the mass of grey I've witnessed on various occasions atop of Mount Snowdon in Wales. Just this time, I was colder. My feet were soaking after hours of walking through deep snow and, had it been an option, I'd have jumped on the first train down from the summit.

We ate lunch as quickly as possible and headed back down. The storm was strengthening faster than we could descend though. The sharp, icy wind stung my teeth as horizontal snow caught on my beard and eyelashes. When we eventually returned to the slightly more sheltered residential streets, we saw the same bull elk, along with another one of slightly smaller stature that was missing half an antler. We wondered if he'd been foolish enough to take on the dominant male.

Having found deer on our doorstep, we were a little disappointed not to have found any on Deer Mountain itself. We later learned this was because the deer migrate to the valley for the winter. It seems only we were stupid enough to spend time at more than 10,000ft in such unforgiving conditions.

Ready for something less exacting, we went into town to visit the Stanley Hotel. Stephen King's one-night stay here in 1974 provided the inspiration for *The Shining*. The hotel bar boasts Colorado's biggest whiskey collection and while whiskey isn't my tipple of choice, we'd had enough frights over the past 24 hours to warrant a stiff drink.

The hotel's white painted wooden siding and red roof makes the building look like it belongs on top of a cake. A fixture on the local tourist trail, I'd anticipated the bar would be full of memorabilia relating to King's book. But with the exception of a small photograph of the author, the bar seemed intent on appearing run-of-the-mill, and the televisions on the wall showed a go-kart race no one was watching. This was a recurring theme in America. Regardless of what was on screen, whether it was poker, wiffle ball (a niche variant of baseball), or rotating adverts about diet pills, TVs in bars were never switched off. It was a strange setting in which to sell whiskey at $1,000-a-glass.

For the first time in my life I was asked whether I wanted my drink neat or on the rocks. The fact I'd reached my early thirties without facing the question hints at a cloistered youth, but I guess I just wasn't hanging out at many whiskey bars. Combined with my earlier achievement of single-handedly pushing a car, the day felt like a rite of passage. I did rather undermine my manliness by ordering a honey-flavoured whiskey, which I suspect purists would regard with the same disdain as James Bond if he was handed a strawberry daiquiri.

We awoke to a white Christmas, which, given the events of recent days, was less exciting than we would otherwise have anticipated. It was our last day of hiking before we left to go skiing and we were determined to make it back into Rocky Mountains National Park. On the advice of our host we set out from the house later than we had the day before, hoping that this time the snow plough would arrive ahead of us.

The forecast had promised sunshine, but the sky remained grey, with the icy wind having the unwelcome effect of giving the numbing -11°C temperature a real feel of -23°C. Seeing the official bright yellow snow ploughs on the streets as we set off was encouraging, but it was the range of wonky, homemade ploughs owners had tagged onto the front of their vehicles that I particularly enjoyed. It made their cars look like they belonged on *Robot Wars*.

Thankfully, most of the fresh snow had been cleared from the road before we arrived in the park. The conditions were still perilous, but at least there was now space to park.

Freelan Stanley, founder of the Stanley Hotel, first visited the area seeking fresh air to aid his recovery from tuberculosis and played an important role in establishing Rocky Mountains National Park. Bear Lake is one of its most celebrated landmarks, and after our two-day struggle to get there, expectations were high. But the sullen sky made the view of the frozen lake appear bleak and it was difficult not to conclude that the lake's stellar reputation was primarily a consequence of its proximity to the car park.

Now equipped with borrowed snowshoes, we continued hiking deeper into the mountains, grateful to be able to follow the fresh tracks of the few people who had been brave enough to arrive before us. Twice the path bisected frozen lakes. Away from the shelter of the trees, I channelled my inner Shackleton as tiny snowflakes whipped across our faces like a burning sea mist.

We weren't surprised to find the top of our water bottle had frozen when we stopped for a picnic at Emerald Lake. The lake is situated directly below Hallett Peak and Flattop Mountain, two summits more than 12,000ft high that form part of the Continental Divide. Along this ridge, raindrops falling only inches apart commence very different journeys, running either west to the Pacific Ocean or east to the Gulf of Mexico and the Atlantic.

Tommy Caldwell and Alex Honnold starred in a documentary released a few months after our visit that depicts their journey along a route Caldwell coined the Continental Divide Ultimate Linkup. The duo climbed Hallett Peak, Flattop Mountain and 15 other summits in the space of just

36 hours. It's easy to see why Caldwell chooses to live nearby.

We retraced our steps to join a loop around more alpine lakes. But, try as we might, we couldn't find the turning. Having fallen waist-deep in the snow, I was ready to give up. Yet from this vantage point I was able to spot the signpost, which had been almost entirely buried by snow.

It quickly became clear how irrelevant this break-through was. No one had hiked along the path for weeks, if not months, and even with the benefit of snowshoes, we sank to our knees at every step. Admitting defeat, we headed back the way we had come to see how far we could travel around the loop in the other direction.

The clouds slowly lifted as the trail ascended through the trees, finally revealing the area's awesome topography. The wind had subsided and with no one else around, the only sound was the clackety-clack of our snowshoes.

We'd promised each other we would be back at the car by 4pm so we could drive out of the park in daylight. The road to hell is paved with good intentions. We were some distance from the car when we saw a sign indicating it was less than a mile to The Loch. People had strongly recom-mended visiting the lake, but we had long since given up hope of reaching it. Throwing caution to the wind, we disre-garded our earlier agreement and picked up the pace. I hope our wedding vows stand up to greater scrutiny.

Neither of us had factored in the climb necessary to reach The Loch. Within 10 minutes I was panting heavily and sweating profusely as my body struggled to adjust to the thin air.

Sarah, striding away up ahead, turned around and looked at me in panic. "Chris!"

I prepared to draw the pole in my left hand behind me to

protect myself from what I assumed could only be an imminent bear attack. "What's wrong?" I asked.

"You look awful."

I wanted to allay her fears, but the truth was that I could barely walk 10 paces without leaning on the nearest tree. I was like a worn-out boxer, clinching in the hope the referee wouldn't notice.

But the referee had noticed. And she was about to call the whole thing off.

"I'm fine, I promise," I said, convincing neither of us.

At this point, a lone hiker walked towards us on his return from The Loch. Judging from the head torch he wore and the nine-inch knife he carried on his hip, he was clearly worried about not making it back in the light.

"Is there anyone else up there?" I asked.

"Not this late in the afternoon there isn't," he replied without breaking step.

The Loch fully justified the effort expended going the distance. All around, tree-covered hillsides gave way to sheer rocky peaks. At the lake I collapsed into the untouched snow and watched in awe as the late afternoon sun broke through the clouds to illuminate the icy mist still falling at higher elevations. Conscious that time was ticking, Sarah switched from referee to trainer, forcing me to swallow an almost frozen energy bar whole.

Then we were on our way, striding back down the mountain. It's amazing how rapidly mild altitude sickness fades when every step is easier on your body than the last. Soon we were running down the shoulder width trail, simulating a bobsleigh as we followed its twists and turns in our race against the clock.

The only thing that slowed our progress was the drama unfolding above our heads. The setting sun cast a transcendent light over the dissipating clouds, reminiscent of the gateway to heaven in a Renaissance painting.

Our reappearance near the trailhead startled the knife-carrying hiker and we departed the park just as the silhouettes of the Rockies faded into the darkness. Back at our accommodation, we treated ourselves to microwaved macaroni cheese for Christmas dinner once again. For what is Christmas without its traditions?

33

INTO THE WILDERNESS PART II:
YOSEMITE

The final few months in California went by in a flash. We were both busy with work, yet we remained keen to make the most of our remaining weekends by visiting some of our favourite places one last time. On the few occasions we did remain close to home, we were dog sitting Spanky. Calling his name in the neighbourhood became normalised worryingly quickly. It was only when Sarah overheard me telling our landlord I wouldn't be at home one afternoon because "I'd be getting Spanky", that I understood why he'd been so willing to suggest a different date.

At the start of May, we vacated our studio and headed south to begin our swansong in the States. The first stop was the town of Mammoth Lakes in the Sierra Nevada, a 30-minute drive south of Mono Lake.

Mammoth Lakes is the last ski resort to close in California each year. Its extended season is possible thanks to the elevation of the mountains, with some runs beginning above 11,000ft. Even to a beginner such as myself, skiing in May felt novel. After skiing in -25°C in Colorado, it was strange in Mammoth Lakes to see car windscreens covered by reflective shields to keep out the heat. They served their purpose though, as temperatures reached 25°C in the after-noon, turning the snow into slush. To mitigate against this, the runs opened at 7.30am, when the overnight freeze created conditions tempting only to ski-starved Brits and international athletes. Like us, the US ski team were in town to make the most of the remaining snow. I wonder what they made of me.

Mammoth, as the area is almost universally called, is home to some of the most spectacular landscapes in America, and Little Lakes Valley boasts, for my money, the best effort to reward ratio of any walk in California. The route gains little more than 1,000ft over eight miles and we were so busy admiring the alpine lakes and 13,000ft glacially scoured peaks, we hardly noticed.

Another day, we were hiking around Lake Mary when we were stopped in our tracks by a sign urging us to turn around as we were about to enter a 'Carbon Dioxide Hazard Area'. When 170 acres of trees died abruptly in the early 1990s, scientists concluded gas was leaking from a newly created underground opening formed by a series of minor earthquakes known as a seismic swarm. As carbon dioxide is heavier than air, it collects in depressions concealed by the snow. There, the concentration of carbon dioxide can be as high as 90%. We didn't feel in imminent danger, but as US Geological Survey scientist Dave Hill told the *LA Times*, "At 70% or 80% [concentration], it just takes a couple of breaths" for the odourless and colourless gas to displace the oxygen in your lungs. The warning sign stated we must "avoid any activity where you could fall face first in the snow". It was just as well I didn't have my skis.

Mammoth Lakes sits directly above Long Valley Caldera, the underground supervolcano responsible for the region's hot springs and quite possibly the future demise of mankind. The most visual reminder of the ticking time-bomb under the surface came in the form of a 10ft wide, 60ft deep fissure running for several hundred feet across the forest. At the bottom, snow would sometimes last all year round, leading generations of Native Americans to use the fissure as a fridge. Rising magma might one day turn it into a cooker, but it's also feasible the fissure will simply fill up with natural debris. The growth of several large trees in the fractured earth indicates the process is already under way.

At the end of the week, we drove towards Yosemite. It was hard to believe during the sweaty journey north, but snow was imminently expected to hit eastern California. While this was a relief to the struggling piste groomers of Mammoth Lakes ski resort, it was rather less welcome news for us. When we had booked our wilderness camping permits six months earlier, we'd pictured the sunny May days of our visit the year before. Not the sight of our breath in sub-zero temperatures.

We stopped for the night in Groveland, a roadside village just outside Yosemite. The colourful wooden porches and worn, corrugated iron roofs evoked Groveland's origins as a gold rush town in the Wild West. Our century-old hotel was built in the same style, and we walked through a dark corridor with low ceilings to reach the reception.

"Are you going somewhere?" asked the manager jovially as he looked at our stuffed backpacks.

We laughed dutifully. "Yosemite bright and early tomorrow."

"You're not camping I hope?"

"We are."

"Rather you than me. It's going to be chilly in the valley."

We knew it was going to be even colder where we were going. "How likely do you think it is to snow?" I asked.

"Normally, not at all at this time of year. Last night I was putting the air con on in the rooms. Tonight I'll be turning on the radiators. If I don't, the guests will be down here demanding extra blankets."

I'd hoped his assessment would provide a little more insight into the region's weather patterns than their impact on the housekeeping.

Changing tack, Sarah tried something more straightforward. "Where do you recommend for dinner?"

"Usually I'd suggest Michoacana, but the owner's on holiday. Opposite is the Iron Door Saloon - the oldest bar in California—"

"That sounds perfect!"

"—though I think I saw a sign saying they aren't doing food today." He thought for a moment. "You could go to Pizza Factory. It's excellent there. But I've heard Dave's sick so they might not be serving food tonight either." He paused once again. "Ooh, you could go to the Hungry Bear."

"Oh yes?"

"It's closed on Sundays though. What day is it?"

"Sunday."

"Ah. That's a shame."

"Is there anywhere that *is* open?" I asked, trying to hide my exasperation.

"Oh yes, lots of places - you just might need to drive 40 minutes."

After a long journey, I wasn't thrilled by the idea, and the option of tucking into one of our dehydrated food packs in our bags was getting more attractive by the minute. Giving up on the conversation, we walked outside to see if we could find anywhere ourselves. We weren't hugely surprised when we did - an independent restaurant called Two Guys. I guess they were three friends short of a franchise.

～

Yosemite Valley looked noticeably different to the previous May. Ice clung to the sides of Upper Yosemite Falls and a smattering of small snowy islands floated downstream. The skies had been reassuringly clear at the start of the day, but it wasn't long before they turned ominously cloudy.

We were to spend five days in the wild. To get to our base camp in Little Yosemite Valley, we ascended the steep path past both Vernal and Nevada Falls. The day hikers we passed watched in admiration as we carried our bags up the mountain, but such ego boosts petered out as we headed deeper into the park. Yosemite extends for more than 1,000 square miles, but nearly a third of all wilderness campers spend time at the campground in Little Yosemite Valley. Thanks in part to the installation of pit toilets and bear lockers, it represents a halfway house between the gift shops and hotels in the valley and truly independent wilderness camping.

As we began to pitch our tent, a squirrel skipped cautiously towards us carrying a clump of dry grass in his mouth that made him look like an east London hipster. He paused so close to Sarah's ankle she could have picked him up. Ground squirrels in Yosemite are famously tame, but this was unusual. Suddenly aware he'd drawn our attention, the bearded squirrel darted down a hole concealed by a nearby rock.

It appeared we had a neighbour building his home, just as we were.

The squirrel's willingness to risk such an encounter soon became clear. Minutes later, heavy snowfall arrived.

We sought refuge by the communal fire. The campground was predominantly empty, suggesting many permit holders had cancelled their plans upon seeing the weather forecast. But this only strengthened our bond with the foolhardy individuals who'd come anyway. Around the fire was

Josh, a student from San Diego, Becca, a girl from Toronto with thick curls of blonde hair and a black smudge across her nose, and Markus, an understated Austrian on his first visit to America. Our conversation took place over the hiss of gas stoves by the crackling fire and the intermittent knocking of a woodpecker attacking a tree trunk like a jack-hammer. Becca and Markus had been in the backcountry for a few days already and we listened eagerly to their reports of the trail conditions - even as they became more redundant by the second.

"I might head up to Merced Lake tomorrow," Josh said.

"If the weather doesn't improve, that was our back-up plan too," I said.

"Maybe we'll be lucky and find some weed."

"Weed?"

"Yeah, a plane crashed up there in the '70s carrying tons of weed from Colombia. When word got out, climbers went up there to salvage it and get high."

This story sounded apocryphal at best. We were all having fun by the fire so it seemed mean-spirited to call it out for the far-fetched fabrication it had to be. I couldn't completely conceal my scepticism though. "Really?"

Becca nodded. "I've heard the same story. They call it Dope Lake."

The next morning I unzipped the tent door and stuck my head out like a curious dormouse on the first day of spring. A dusting of snow lay on the ground, showing Yosemite as we had never seen it before. Up above, Half Dome was shrouded in sunlit mist. The landmark soars directly above the campground in Little Yosemite Valley, but the heavy clouds of the previous evening had obscured any sight of it.

Not everyone was as impressed by the wintry transfor-mation of the forest. A few campers who had chosen to stay sheltering in their tents when the snow arrived were now irritably trying to get the ice out of their water bottles.

We took the tent down amidst another flurry of snow. In the time it took us to fold up the tent and put it in my rucksack, the rectangle of exposed ground showing where we had slept had all but disappeared. We quickly decided to adopt Plan B. After failing to find Josh, we began following the Merced River upstream to Dope Lake.

A narrow path took us through the dark forest until it opened up unexpectedly. We had arrived at the burn zone of the 2014 Meadow Fire. Falling snow contrasted against a backdrop of thousands of blackened tree carcasses. Only birds had returned to the wasteland and the sound of our approach caused robins, red winged black birds and bright yellow western tanagers to all take flight to neighbouring tree stumps.

The weather alternated between periods of sun and snow in a similar pattern to the speed of the river as it flowed downstream. As we ascended, the sunshine, like the calm stretches of water, became more sporadic, replaced by settling snow and thunderous rapids.

In a 1930 report for the US Department of the Interior, Francois Matthes described the monoliths either side of us as "exceptionally massive". He meant this in the strictly geological sense, in that the rocks are without internal structure or layers and are homogeneous in composition, but the phrase's more common meaning is just as valid. Seasonal waterfalls cascaded hundreds of metres down the smooth, rounded granite surfaces towards the Merced River.

Lunch was consumed in a blizzard. As a result of the lack of space in the bear canister, it was a spartan affair consisting of wraps filled with cheese and carrots. The pre-sliced cheese was the same colour as the rounded carrot batons, and the lurid monochrome had the appearance of a meal prepared by a toddler. It made a change at least from the peanut butter wraps of our previous wilderness trip.

At the edge of Merced Lake we were surprised to come across barred wooden huts and half-built metal frames next to sealed off taps and a fire pit covered in snow. The lake looked even bleaker and it would have taken more than marijuana to tempt me in. Not that there was any evidence of a crash landing. Subsequent research explained why. It wasn't because the event never happened, but because we were seven miles north of the lake where it did. Far from being a yarn that had been embellished over the years with each retelling, Josh and Becca had in fact underplayed the events at Lower Merced Pass Lake, which truly are stranger than fiction.

When an employee at the Ahwahnee Hotel stumbled upon the wreckage in January 1977 and reported the number printed on the wing, the DEA (the US Drug Enforcement Administration) instantly became suspicious. However, the recovery of the bodies and the suspected high value cargo would be a slow process. Years later, the park service's lead diver, Butch Farabee, told *Men's Journal* the operation took place in the worst conditions he'd ever seen. The leaking aviation fuel and hydraulic fluids turned the water murky, making it even more challenging to avoid the twisted metal frozen in the ice. The marijuana floating near the surface was taken away as evidence, but further progress was halted by the imminent arrival of a major storm.

Officials believed access to the backcountry would be cut off by the storm, so the crime scene was vacated until work could resume. Rumours had begun to spread in the valley though, where a group of 20 hardcore hippy climbers known as the Stonemasters were living. These were the best big-wall climbers in the world and would sometimes be called upon by the rangers for assistance during difficult search and rescue operations. As park ranger Tim Setnicka later admitted, "We underestimated the entrepreneurial spirit of certain members of the community." Armed with their knowledge of the Yosemite Wilderness - and 'borrowed' axes and chainsaws - they travelled to the site, removing more than a hundred bales of marijuana over the course of three months.

Within weeks Yosemite was awash with weed laced with aviation fuel, which made it prone to spark and crackle when smoked. Park rangers suspected something was afoot when the previously hand-to-mouth climbing community started dropping $100 tips in the Ahwahnee Hotel and local scuba diving companies reported an unexpected surge in demand for rental equipment.

The story is still celebrated for the plucky ingenuity and determination of a ragtag bunch of misfits, but by this point, word had spread across California. Tension grew at the lake as drug dealers and hustlers who'd never been to Yosemite before tried to stake their claim.

Embarrassed by the crash site's growing notoriety, in April 1977 the authorities reclaimed the site by force, sending everyone scarpering into the woods to avoid jail sentences. From that point on, rangers remained at the site to turn away any opportunists.

The fuselage remained in the lake until June, when the conditions finally allowed a full recovery operation to take place. By this point, almost all of the 2.7 tonnes (6,000 lbs) of marijuana originally held in the plane had disappeared. No one was ever convicted in relation to its disappearance. Some of the most resourceful climbers reportedly sold their loot for more than $20,000 ($100,000 in today's money) each. One paid for his college education with the proceeds. Another bought a house. I wonder whether they were more worried about the IRS finding out or their fellow hippies.

At Merced Lake, we were cheered by the arrival of another bedraggled couple, followed not long afterwards by Josh. The temperature hadn't risen above freezing the whole day and we collectively set about lighting a fire as quickly as we could. Huddled next to the smoke pouring out of the wet wood, it was all but impossible to tell the difference between falling snowflakes and burning embers. Not only was it disconcerting, it created fresh holes in my jeans.

We retired to our tent to find it had turned into an igloo. Our breath was clearly visible inside the canvas and we hastily jumped into our sleeping bags with everything but our anoraks on. Merced Lake is 7,250ft above sea level and overnight the temperatures fell to -11°C. This represented an impressive 49°C swing from the daytime peak recorded during our adventure in Hetch Hetchy, our previous wilderness camping experience in Yosemite.

We awoke to beautiful sunshine and a clear blue sky. Not that we'd known from inside the tent, where it had been kept artificially dark by the thick covering of snow. Our boots, which we'd brought inside overnight, showed no sign of thawing, which at least meant there weren't pools of water in the tent.

To avoid disassembling the tent in the severe cold, we first walked three miles to Washburn Lake. We followed coyote footprints for so long, I began to worry we'd misplaced the trail and were about to present ourselves at its door for breakfast. Around us, snowflakes fell in bursts from the sagging branches, catching the sunlight that peeked between the thick trunks. Elsewhere, only the fastest flowing water in the river's central channel remained in motion. Xylophone-shaped rows of icicles hung from exposed tree roots on the riverbank, resembling an entrance to a mystical subterranean cavern.

The granite mountains next to the lake looked like they

had been doused in icing sugar. We admired their reflection in the still water, before returning to collect our tent. We then continued descending back towards Little Yosemite Valley, past melting icicles swinging like pendulums in the warm air.

To our relief, the weather held and no further snow arrived so the following morning we headed to Clouds Rest. At almost 10,000ft, the summit is considered by many to possess the best view in the park. In a land of such breathtaking beauty this is quite a claim. My familiar difficulties with altitude returned once again and halfway up I welcomed the chance to catch my breath when I was distracted by the impatient howls of wolf pups in the nearby bushes.

At the top, snowy peaks stretched into the distance in all directions. Many lay beyond Yosemite's perimeter, in Ansel Adams Wilderness and Inyo National Forest. Looking north-east, Lake Tenaya was easily identifiable next to the Tioga Pass, which remained empty as it hadn't yet reopened for the season. To the south-west stood Half Dome and Yosemite Valley. Nonetheless, at nearly 6,000ft above the valley floor, we felt too far away from the action. Climbing to Clouds Rest earns hikers bragging rights, but there are better views elsewhere in the park.

Turning our backs to the valley, we continued our loop by walking along a snowy ridge that dropped off precipitously. Above us, a solar halo - the daytime equivalent of the phenomenon we'd spotted in Zion - was on display. Perhaps it's a national park thing.

We descended back into the valley of fallen trees created by the 2014 Meadow Fire. From the hillside, they looked like used matchsticks: burned, shrivelled and severed. Clambering over them left charcoal marks across our hands and clothes as the outer layer of the trees crumbled under our touch. Belatedly, we understood where the black smudge on Becca's nose had come from.

Just before we arrived at the campground, we saw a black bear run across our path. He paid us no attention and began tearing bark off a fallen tree with the ease of a child ripping open wrapping paper.

Little Yosemite Valley's popularity with first time wilderness campers has contributed to the campground gaining a regrettable reputation for bear sightings. The bears, attracted by the easy access to food yielded by careless weekenders, simply can't resist. We heard how one hiker had slathered himself in Deep Heat and awoke from a nap to find himself nose to nose with a curious bear.

We set off from the campground at 6:40 the following morning to be among the first to the summit of Half Dome. Our experience of the crowded chaos at Angels Landing had taught us it would be less stressful knowing a fatal fall would be our own doing.

During the summer months metal posts connected by cables are installed and wooden boards are placed on the rock face to assist hikers. At least 13 people have died on this 'path' since 2005, but access permits to the route remain one of the most sought-after tickets in the country.

Our ascent was out of season, so we didn't need a permit, but it meant we would be climbing when the cables were down and before the wooden boards and metal posts were in place. This is not encouraged by park officials. Nevertheless, as a ranger at the campground admitted the night before, "Now's the time to do it. Conditions are good and there aren't many people." We declined to remind him of the blizzard just three days earlier.

This was one challenge we weren't taking lightly. We'd followed advice on website forums and packed gloves, harnesses and ropes, and Sarah had watched YouTube videos to learn how to make Prusik knots that would - we hoped - catch us if we fell.

After climbing the steps to the top of Sub Dome, we stood alone on the 8,400ft ridge that connected it to Half Dome and looked up towards the final ascent. Sarah began to coolly unpack the bags of climbing equipment she had pre-prepared, while I fretted that our belongings were about to slide off the edge. Surveying the laid out kit, I struggled to hold back my rising panic.

"Why do you have a blue rope? I don't have one! Do I need one?"

"I ran out of blue rope. You have three yellow ropes instead," Sarah replied. "But you can have the blue one if you want."

I went back to trying to put my climbing harness on over my jeans.

Just as I realised I'd put my harness on inside out, a German man in his early thirties arrived.

As he absent-mindedly adjusted his professional-looking via ferrata climbing gear, he looked up and said, "Do you want to exchange phones so we can take photographs of each other during the climb?"

I couldn't even pretend to entertain the idea. The thoughtful suggestion overlooked the fact I hadn't gone climbing for nearly twenty years. "Err...I'd love to, but I just don't think I'll be able to, sorry." I didn't trust myself not to drop my own phone, never mind anyone else's.

"Ok, no problem. Do you want me to take some pictures on yours anyway?"

After his show of faith in my non-existent climbing skills, it felt churlish to question his.

"That's very kind, thank you," I said, trying to hide my reservations as I handed over my phone. "We'll take lots of photos of you when we get to the top."

The German began climbing and was far above us when he shouted down an apology that it was too steep for him to take any photographs. Which was, in a perverse way, a slight comfort.

We attached our rope to the metal cable on the ground and began pulling ourselves up the rock face. Every 30 metres the line of cable would end and we had to fasten ourselves to the next section and detach from the previous. This required tying a new knot each time and necessitated going hands-free as I nervously fiddled with the rope and opened the carabiner. Just the grip of my hiking boots kept me anchored. If I slipped, I was relying on the efficacy of the knot I'd made a minute earlier. Each time, I worried I had tied the rope incorrectly and that, when put to the test, it would unravel faster than a toddler's fib. I'd only learn of my error as I plunged 4,000ft to the valley floor.

Brief glances over my shoulder showed the view was sublime. Yet I couldn't pause for long in case my brain began to process the danger. So I kept my head down most of the time and looked on in envy as a lizard ran effortlessly up the rock.

Sarah may lack my upper body strength, but any advantage this gave me was negated by the fact she was unencumbered by a fear of heights. She waited near the top and we reached the summit together, breathless but exalted.

Despite my misgivings, the ascent was worth it. We could see straight down Yosemite Valley, across to Glacier Point, and by turning around, look up towards Clouds Rest. To our surprise, we also spotted a waterfall we hadn't seen before. Measuring more than 2,000ft high, Snow Creek Waterfall is the second tallest waterfall in the park, and thus one of the largest in the world. However, it's little-known as the cascade is concealed by the surrounding topography and Half Dome's summit is one of the few places from which its scale can be observed.

Patches of snow remained at the peak and while the German posed for photos with his legs dangling precariously over the edge, I was reluctant to fully relax until we'd returned down the cables. As expected, the number of climbers had increased during our time at the top. This created the fresh challenge of having to pass them while sharing the cable.

One man, breathing hard from the climb's intensity, described the ascent as "a bit spicy", while another gaily proclaimed that "these are the moments you live for". I could only muster a half-hearted smile in response. This was more than the next person we encountered could manage though. A panic attack had brought her to a tearful standstill and she was cursing her husband for telling her there wasn't anything to worry about. The faces of the people below her suggested otherwise.

Having climbed Half Dome once, I've no wish to do so again. I'd learned I was not someone who enjoys climbing, but rather someone who enjoys having climbed.

34

INTO THE WILDERNESS PART III: KINGS CANYON AND SEQUOIA NATIONAL PARK

The next day we replenished our supplies and drove to the edge of Kings Canyon National Park, ready to begin another four days of hiking. This time we would be following Rae Lake's Loop, an acclaimed route considered by many to incorporate the most beautiful section of the Pacific Crest Trail. The park's canyon is deeper than the Grand Canyon and the walk starts at the bottom of it. It then ascends rapidly for 23 miles to 12,000ft at Glen Pass. The recent snowfall had put our ambitions in serious jeopardy. 12,000ft was more than 2,000ft higher than Clouds Rest and 1,000ft higher than the highest point at the ski resort in Mammoth. We could only fit four days' supply of rations in our bear canister, so it was essential we found out by the start of Day 3 whether we could make it over Glen Pass. If we couldn't, we'd have to turn on our heels and begin the dispiriting journey back to the car.

Rivers run along the length of the route and the countless waterfalls we passed were in full flow. Initially, we asked anyone coming the other way for information about the conditions at higher levels, but we soon gave up as no one had tried to reach them. At the visitor centre, they hadn't been able to tell us anything either, as none of the rangers had ventured up there since the previous autumn.

We spent the first night at Upper Paradise Valley campground. While we waited by the river for the appearance of that night's blood supermoon, we spotted on the opposite bank a concrete block attached to a flight of wooden stairs leading nowhere.

"Are you looking for a way across?" asked a voice from behind us.

We turned around to see two hulking figures coming out of the woods towards us. Both were in their forties. Neither appeared to possess a neck.

"No, we're just enjoying the river," Sarah replied. "Isn't there a bridge?

"There was," he said, pointing to the stairs. "Was washed away in 2017."

"Oh." The river was approximately eight metres wide and our view of the large, rounded stones in the channel suggested the water was no more than shin-deep. If this sounds like we could have waded across, the flow of the snowmelt swelled river indicated otherwise.

"Didn't you know? We've been worried about this for months."

They walked off downstream to find an alternative crossing, so Sarah and I explored upstream. After a hard day of hiking, we were desperate to know there was a way across. Someone, we reasoned, must have used a makeshift bridge to cross the river since 2017. But all four of us failed to find anywhere even remotely suitable and we began to suspect our arrival in late spring had coincided with the only time of year the crossing was hazardous. By the time we reconvened it was getting dark. The blood supermoon remained as elusive as a passage over the water and I realised with disappointment the moon was blocked by the mountains around us. We conceded defeat and went to bed, hoping the new day would bring better luck.

As I stumbled out of our tent, one of the burly men delivered good news.

"There's a fallen tree spanning both banks 'bout 15 minutes upstream," he said. "Dunno if my partner will go for it though. It looks a bit hairy."

He wasn't wrong.

Sharp, broken branches jutted out at all angles from the narrow tree trunk. The river was significantly wider here and it was difficult to ignore the white water surging beneath our feet as we tottered under the weight of our heavy backpacks. We knew one wrong step would leave us with a lot more than a wet sleeping bag to worry about.

The relief at having made it across was short-lived. Our attempts to find the path again were hampered by thick undergrowth, marshland and a succession of tributaries. When we finally rejoined the path, we were met by a large orange, white and brown snake we later identified as a California mountain kingsnake. We didn't see our fellow campers again.

Butterflies danced in the sunlight and the ravine reverberated with the pulsating soundtrack of hundreds of cicadas and bright yellow crickets. After climbing for some time, we arrived above a sweeping alpine meadow. The views of the pine trees, scattered moraine and lush grassland made it feel like we were stepping into an Evian advert.

Beyond the meadow was a stock crossing. How we could have done with one of these a few hours before. We sat on the smoothed pebbles of the riverbank and ate wraps filled with vacuum-packed salmon. In comparison to the carrots and cheese wraps we'd eked out in Yosemite, this felt like the height of luxury and was thanks to a company having the poor judgement to identify me as a social media influencer. I suspect my post promoting the product left my 1,000 followers bemused rather than inspired, but it was a treat for us. Selling out has never tasted so good.

We crossed an elaborately engineered suspension bridge to the other side of the river. The sudden upgrade in amenities signalled that we'd joined up with both the John Muir Trail (JMT) and the Pacific Crest Trail (PCT). Here, we were less than 40 miles from the end of the JMT, which runs from Yosemite to Mount Whitney, the highest peak in the United States outside of Alaska. It was too early in the season to see people finishing the route, but we did meet hikers walking the PCT in the opposite direction.

We asked a group of unshaven men in their thirties how they had fared on Glen Pass. We soon wished we hadn't.

"It's gnarly up there. Jonno lost a pole and Brad lost a boot." The thought of having to walk hundreds of miles with only one shoe until I reached the nearest shop sounded dreadful. The alarm must have showed on my face, for he quickly added, "He's got it back now. We had to dig for it as he lost it when he sank up to his thigh in the snow. Dunno where Jonno's pole is," he added with a shrug. "It slipped on the ice and skated a few hundred feet down the mountain."

"Well, at least you got the shoe back," I said, trying to remain upbeat. "The pass is doable though?"

"Yeah, just about. You've got ice picks right?"

"No." It hadn't even crossed our minds to get some. We were going for a nice walk, not trying to kill Trotsky.

"But you've got crampons?"

"Kind of. We've got microspikes. We don't have poles though."

"No poles?" He looked doubtful. "Well, rather you than me."

These rugged men didn't appear to be the type to scare

easily and as we walked on I found it difficult to disregard the suspicion it wouldn't be long before we were back.

We had felt pretty hardcore racking up the miles through blizzards in the preceding days. But our achievements were put into perspective by those around us. Only around half of those who set out on the 2,650-mile journey to Canada complete it, and looking at the contrasting emotions of the few people who passed us, it was clear that for some, hiking the PCT had turned into a relentless slog.

When we asked one lone woman in her early twenties how much further she had to go, she said simply "four months". Another woman passed us, hunched as if she was walking into a gale. She looked to be having a terrible time. I doubt she even knew we were there and was certainly oblivious to the splendour of the landscape she was walking through. It was like she'd gone to the cinema, but had chosen to resolutely look at her shoes for the duration of the film.

But who were we to judge? We were just part-timers, critiquing those who had already spent two months carrying heavier rucksacks than the ones on our shoulders. Sarah wasn't quite as easily dissuaded, but as much as I like hiking, I could tell the PCT was not for me.

Happily, we did meet some more cheerful trail companions.

"Hey, where have you guys dropped in from?" asked an attractive woman with brown hair. She was part of a group of eight twenty-somethings, all wearing matching grey T-shirts.

"Err...Kings Canyon," I replied, feeling like an imposter. "What about you?"

"Well, we started in Mexico and kept going!"

"And you made it over Glen Pass ok?"

"Yeah. But it was the hardest part of the trail so far."

"We don't have ice picks, so we're worried we might not be able to do it," Sarah said.

"Do you need to cross the pass today?"

"No, we're planning on doing it tomorrow morning."

"You might be alright then. The other side of the mountain - the one we climbed up - doesn't have much snow on it, so if you get to the summit you'll be fine. Thing is, it doesn't take long for the snow to start melting in the sunshine, and if you get the timing wrong you won't make it. But the snow will freeze overnight, so if you start climbing just before dawn, it'll be solid enough to walk on and you'll have enough light to avoid the pot holes we created coming down."

"Thanks. That sounds so much better than what we heard from the people just ahead of you."

"There's people just ahead of us?"

They hadn't met any fellow PCT hikers for several days and it was heartening to see how excited they were to learn others were nearby. The need to tackle Glen Pass early in the day had evidently created an accordion effect on thru-hiker traffic.

Buoyed by each other's news, we pushed on.

Our progress slowed considerably when we reached the snowline. Here, at almost exactly 10,000ft, any visible sections of the path turned into a river. The parts that remained cloaked in snow had become slushy in the afternoon sun and each step was a gamble as to whether the snow underfoot would be solid enough to bear our weight. When it wasn't, we plunged straight through onto the rocks 3ft below. The fragility of my ankles and our isolated location only heightened the risk.

To our relief, the snow thinned and the climb plateaued, albeit temporarily, at Dollar Lake. Over the three miles that followed, we passed Arrowhead Lake and the Rae Lakes that give the route its name. On our right were the peaks of the Sierra Nevada. The most eye-catching was Fin Dome, a spike of granite named in 1899 by a man called Bolton Brown. To him, the trail around the lakes resembled a sea serpent. The jutting rock represented the monster's fin and Glen Pass its head. Several years earlier, Brown had established the art department at Stanford University. However, his days on campus were numbered and he was fired in 1902 after a long-running dispute over his use of nude models in the classroom.

The sun was gradually beginning to disappear behind the mountains as we approached the foot of Glen Pass. Around us, rotund yellow-bellied marmots were eating the recently thawed patches of grass. They paid us little attention as we strode past towards Upper Rae Lake. Its surface was covered almost entirely by ice, but where it had begun to recede, fish could be seen swimming and the perfect reflection of the peaks looked like a gateway into a parallel universe. We pitched our tent close by and ate dinner in awed silence as the light faded from the sky.

We couldn't have asked for more favourable conditions the following morning. The snow had frozen overnight as we had hoped and the air, though gaspingly cold, was still. Watching the sunlight catch the summits more than 1,500ft above us, I felt confident. If we could climb Half Dome, we could do this too. But while the route to the top of Half Dome had been relatively obvious, snow obscured the switchbacks leading towards Glen Pass.

We followed the haphazard frozen tracks of those who had gone before, but there was no sign of the missing pole. The ice made the tracks slippery and often required us to scramble on our hands and knees, but this was far better than falling through the melting snow.

After 90 minutes of climbing we reached the pass and

celebrated in jubilant relief that we wouldn't have to turn back. Peering over the boulder and scree-littered ridge, I was reassured to see the south side of the mountain was, as promised, less snowy. With a long, last lingering look down over Rae Lakes, we began the 2,500ft descent to Vidette Meadow. We paused frequently along the way to admire captivating frozen alpine lakes and the panoramic mountain views of East Vidette on the opposite side of the valley.

Deer grazed contentedly in the meadow's wetlands as snow water rushed to join Bubbs Creek. Looking out at them while we ate lunch, it was difficult to believe we were barely 25 miles due west of Death Valley.

Over the next two days we followed the creek virtually all the way back to the car at Road's End. Amid the awesome views, bright red phallic buds poked through the bed of pine cones around us. The plant's name, *Sarcodes sanguinea*, loosely translates as 'the bloody flesh-like thing'. The species is a parasite that feeds off tree roots and, as such, doesn't need sunlight to survive. Less vampiric in their appeal were the woolly mule ears growing along the path. Unlike in Tahoe, where we had seen them looking desiccated in late July, the sunflower-like displays of the earliest bloomers were on show, drawing attention to the incredibly soft leaves that give the plant its name.

After a final night in the tent, we began the hour-long drive back to the entrance gate of the park. As the sun rose above the canyon, it illuminated the bright yellow St John's Wort flowers on the side of the road. Beyond them were the shadowed layers of the backlit mountains we had spent the past few days climbing.

From the main gate we continued driving along Generals Highway through neighbouring Sequoia National Park. Fire had torn through the forest the previous year and dead trees extended for miles into the distance. Visitors still queued to have their photograph taken under the park entrance sign, regardless of the charred remains in the background.

Fire is essential to the life cycle of giant sequoias. Seeds are only released when its pine cones become hot and open up. Traditionally, fires in sequoia forests burn low to the ground and produce *relatively* moderate heat, enabling mature sequoias to survive, while killing thinner barked species competing for sunlight and water. But recent wild-fires have been different. A combination of parched vegetation and an accumulation of forest debris is making fires hotter and fuelling the flames higher into the canopy. Fears that the fire that ripped through the national park would destroy the world's largest tree led firefighters to cover its base with fire blankets.

General Sherman's status may see it receive special treatment, but in many ways it's overshadowed by other world-leading trees. It tops out nearly 30% lower than the Hyperion tree and is approximately 1,000 years younger than the oldest living sequoia. Yet the fact it has more wood in its trunk than any other tree on the planet has made it the world's most famous. After all, size matters.

It has no hope of catching the Hyperion as it's no longer growing taller. Like most of the ageing tourists visiting the tree though, it hasn't stopped getting wider. The tree's girth is currently 33 metres at ground level and if the trunk was filled with water, it would fill almost 10,000 baths. Staring up at the tree, it was difficult to imagine the size of the coastal redwood that fell in northern California in 1905, which is estimated to have contained nearly twice the volume of General Sherman.

We resumed driving south, passing the oil pumps that populate the dry open plains as we headed for the coast.

35

THE CHANNEL ISLANDS

I'd told Sarah we wouldn't need to worry about the weather once we'd travelled further south and we had planned to spend the next day recuperating on the beach. But June Gloom, as Santa Barbara locals call the fog that rolls in from the ocean at this time of year, was already out in force. Instead, we entertained ourselves on the pier watching pelicans eat cast-offs from fishermen. The silhouette of each fish could be seen desperately flopping around inside the pouch of the birds' bills, before the pelicans tilted their heads back, sending the helpless fish sliding down their gullet.

The following morning we departed for the Channel Islands. Known as 'California's Galapagos', the chain of eight islands is home to 145 plant and animal species found nowhere else in the world. The oldest human remains in North America were discovered here too and are estimated to be 13,000 years old.

Our destination was Santa Cruz, the largest island in California, and one of the five that make up the state's only offshore national park. Soon after the tall palm trees on the mainland disappeared from view, stripy white and grey dolphins began jumping through the water next to the boat.

When two enormous humpback whales also came into view, the boat schedule was disregarded to follow them. This was an unexpected thrill, but it turned our already ambitious hike to the campsite on the other side of the island into a race against the sun.

When battling through the snow by Rae Lakes, we had fantasised that Santa Cruz's location 20 miles off the south Californian coast might give it the appearance of a desert island. Such hopes evaporated upon seeing the rolling hills of scorched yellow grassland.

We landed at Prisoners Harbour. A beleaguered Danish captain called Andrew Christian Holmes docked here nearly 200 years before. He had been instructed to transport 80 prisoners from Acapulco in Mexico to mainland California, but he was refused entry to the destination. Unsure where to turn, he gave 30 of the worst convicts some supplies and left them at Santa Cruz island. It wasn't long before the men resolved to leave. Whether they made it to the mainland is uncertain, with some reports indicating they returned on makeshift rafts and others suggesting they died attempting to do so.

Five years later and 50 miles away, on another of the Channel Islands, the Nicoleño Native American tribe were being forcibly removed. In the commotion, a woman in her early thirties, later known as Juana Maria, was left behind. She lived alone on the island for 18 years, surviving on shellfish and seal fat, until she was found and brought to the mainland by a hunter. In Santa Barbara Juana Maria was able to communicate only with the few remaining members of her tribe, but was reportedly delighted by the sight of horses and European food. Her story, sadly, does not have a happy ending. She died from dysentery just seven weeks later.

After a sweaty walk uphill we hiked along the island's

spine, passing prickly pear cacti and resilient, flowering pink succulents on the way up Mount Diablo. The peak is the highest point on the Channel Islands, and although its elevation is nearly five times lower than Glen Pass, it's only a couple of hundred metres smaller than England's greatest summit.

As we descended towards Scorpion Cove, the early evening sun lit up dandelions with grey seed heads the size of fists. I assumed this was one of the islands' endemic species, but purple salsify is an invasive plant introduced by missionaries, hunters and ranchers.

Just ahead of us, an island fox jumped out of the long grass and onto the path. The animal is the most famous of the islands' endemic species and is the same size as a cat. The foxes found here are the smallest in North America and their diminutive size is a consequence of insular dwarfism, which causes animals to become smaller as they evolve, partly in response to the size and availability of their prey.

The novelty of the sighting diminished when we reached the campsite, where three more miniature foxes hovered as we ate dinner in the darkness. It goes to show, you can take a fox anywhere and it will still be found lurking around populated areas, ever ready for an easy meal.

The foxes themselves became an easy meal in the 1990s. For the first time, golden eagles four times their size began breeding on the islands, decimating the fox population. This led to renewed efforts to increase the number of nesting bald eagles, as they keep golden eagles at bay and predominantly eat fish. We saw two flying by the clifftop as we left on the ferry the next day. Judging by the lack of golden eagles we saw on the island, the conservation efforts appear to be working.

36

LOS ANGELES

From one of the most isolated places in California, to one of the most visited. When we arrived in LA, we headed straight to the Hollywood sign at Griffith Park. Erected in 1923 as a temporary advertisement for a local housing development, the 'Hollywoodland' sign only adopted its shortened form 26 years later. Since then, protestors and pranksters have modified the sign to read alternative variations including 'Hollyweed', 'Oil War' and 'Jollygood'.

From Dante's Peak, we could see Griffith Observatory sitting below us on the southern slope of Mount Hollywood. Beyond it, a cluster of skyscrapers dominated a horizon otherwise obscured by polluted haze. We descended reluctantly, knowing the time had come to sell our beloved car.

Los Angeles was the final destination of our adventure in America and the hot, hellish journey through the city's congested roads reaffirmed the pressing need to sell the Pontiac. We received a cheque for nearly half of the $2,000 we had bought it for, which, considering the hard yards it had done, and the fact it had been making a horribly disconcerting grinding noise every time we braked since we departed Yosemite, didn't seem too bad.

Our sadness at saying goodbye to the vehicle was alleviated by being picked up from the garage in arguably the most quintessentially American car on the road. Travelling in a brand new Ford F-150 made for an entertaining journey and our Uber driver enjoyed our awed reactions to the truck's many features. The car has been the best-selling vehicle in the States for four decades. When the motoring website PistonHeads tested the F-150 on UK roads, it described the experience as "diverting, but never less than hard work". This was equally true in Los Angeles. Frankly, it's a preposterous car to use for ferrying strangers around a city.

For a start, the truck drinks fuel faster than the city's population syphons water from Lake Mono. Its wing mirrors were larger than my head and the car was so wide, the gap between the two front seats was bigger than some of the chairs found on budget airlines. While passing a Land Rover, I sensed we could have driven straight over the top of it. This truck might be destroying the planet, but it indisputably makes you king of the road.

We were staying by the coast in LA, in a stylish neighbourhood within the Venice Canals. Its quiet streets were interconnected by footbridges over waterways reflecting colourful houses and palm trees in the front gardens. The tranquility of this residential area was offset by the liveliness of the nearby Venice Beach boardwalk. In place of the floating kayaks and primitive rowing boats of the canals were tattoo parlours, food counters and souvenir shops. But unless you have a girlfriend looking for tiny shorts emblazoned with derogatory slogans, don't come here for the shopping.

Venice Beach is one of the best places to people watch on the planet. Individuals from all walks of life can be found here, from affluent property owners, to the homeless, and from dubious junkies to gym-goers honing their physiques on adjacent Muscle Beach. This is a place where a woman rollerblading down the street in just a bikini doesn't warrant a second thought. Neither does the man 'singing' *Surfin' USA* in a loud monotone voice, or the forty-something drinking coffee and taking a business call while skateboarding in dungarees.

Early the next morning we returned to the boardwalk on bikes borrowed from our accommodation. En route we passed a man in a wetsuit walking back from the beach, as quickly as his bare feet and surfboard would permit, in readiness for the start of the working day. Most of the shops' metal shutters were down on the boardwalk and few other people were about. Yet the sea breeze still carried the unmistakable smell of marijuana.

As we cycled around the bay, my eyes were drawn to the promenade's street art. Much of it was dedicated to the veneration of deceased LA Lakers star Kobe Bryant. After a brief pit stop at Muscle Beach to climb the ropes before the zealots arrived, we continued past Santa Monica pier to reach the Getty Villa. At the entrance to the grounds we were greeted by a sign stating:

> All visitors must park at the Villa or arrive by bus or taxi. We regret that pedestrians are not allowed.

Small wonder LA has a traffic problem. The unwelcome nature of our arrival threw the security guard, who insisted on calling a private bus for us to ride 30 seconds from the entrance gate to the front door of the villa.

The landmark is the culmination of an extraordinary effort - one might say folly - by oil tycoon Jean Paul Getty to recreate the luxurious Villa dei Papiri in the Bay of Naples in Italy. Believed to have once been owned by the father-in-law of Julius Caesar, the building was buried by the erup-tion of Mount Vesuvius in 79 AD.

Getty never visited his completed villa, but it is a testa-ment to what can be created when passion is combined with unimaginable wealth. The museum holds 44,000 Greek, Roman and Etruscan artefacts at its opulent hillside loca-tion overlooking the Pacific Ocean. It's also home to a 67-metre-long pool in the centre of the garden, surrounded by replicas of statues excavated from the original villa.

Getty's attempt to turn back time to showcase the beauty of the antiquities as they were created, rather than as ancient, weathered ruins, feels like the Disneyfication of history. The villa is the physical embodiment of the scene at the end of *Beauty and the Beast*, where the spell is lifted and the beauty of the castle is revealed anew.

It's an unfortunate paradox that some of the efforts made to achieve historical accuracy undermine the credi-bility of the endeavour. For example, the bronze statues by the pool all had painted eyes, which is how they would have looked during the Papiri's heyday. The tendency for paint to flake off over time though has led society today to associate classical statues with blank eyes. For this reason, the painted irises and pupils seemed odd and every statue looked like someone who had just realised they'd locked their keys in the car.

A few months earlier, friends from the UK were lucky enough to be in Yosemite at the time of the Firefall. This natural phenomenon is created when the setting sun perfectly illuminates Horsetail Fall, briefly making the waterfall glow red and orange. It doesn't happen every year, and as impressed as they were by the event, it was the hollering and whooping of the elated, predominantly Amer-ican crowd that they particularly enjoyed. Likewise, while it was interesting to stroll around Getty's modern day Roman palace, it was the antics of the other visitors that stood out. We watched from the balcony as couples and groups of girls took selfie after selfie in various coquettish poses around the garden. Some had even brought a range of outfits. I wondered how many Instagrammers had claimed the villa as their own and what Jean Paul Getty would have made of it all.

After nearly two years in California, our time had come to an end. We were disappointed not to have made it to the state's two remaining national parks: Joshua Tree NP and Lassen Volcanic NP. But in a state that is larger than 85 countries, we were always unlikely to see everything we wanted to. One day we will come back.

Hopefully, they'll still be serving cab sav.

ACKNOWLEDGMENTS

Obviously, this book wouldn't have been possible without Sarah. I was the luckiest trailing spouse alive. Since returning to the UK, Sarah has continued to provide vital, unstinting support by jogging my memory when required and by dedicating many hours to helping me make the book as good as it could be.

I would also like to thank Kim and Sally at Off Grid for the excellent book cover and map of California. The cover image is a modified version of a photograph I took of Sarah at Glen Pass on Rae Lakes Loop, and it's a memory I will always cherish.